Writing Toward the Light

A Grief Journey

by Laura Flett

Eagle Wings Press
Imprint of Silver Boomer Books
Abilene, Texas

Scripture quotation marked NRSV from: New Revised Standard Version Bible, copyright © 1989, Division of Christian Education of the National Council of the Churches of Christ in the United States of America. Used by permission. All rights reserved.

Scripture marked NKJV taken from the New King James Version. Copyright © 1982 by Thomas Nelson, Inc. Used by permission. All rights reserved.

Writing Toward The Light: A Grief Journey, copyright © 2009, Laura Flett.

A previous version *Writing Toward the Light: a Mother's Grief Journey*, copyright © 2008 by Laura Flett.

Published by Eagle Wings Press, an imprint of Silver Boomer Books, 3301 S 14th Suite 16 - PMB 134, Abilene TX 79606

Picture "Love Letters" on front cover, copyright © Naffarts | Dreamstime.com

Other cover art, copyright © 2009 by Silver Boomer Books

Photographs, copyright © 2009 by the owner, used by permission.

www.EagleWingsPress.com
Imprint of Silver Boomer Books
~§~
SilverBoomerBooks@gmail.com

ISBN: 978-0-9802120-3-7

And a woman who held a babe against
her bosom said, Speak to us of Children.

And he said:
Your children are not your children.
They are the sons and daughters of
    Life's longing for itself.
They come through you but not from
    you,
And though they are with you yet they
    belong not to you.

The Prophet
by Kahlil Gibran

Table of Contents

Preface

My precious son Carlton died. He was the Light of my life, and I was plunged into darkness. I desperately needed to know what happened to him. His life force was no longer contained in an earth body. Where did he go? Who am I now? What is our relationship to be? I began an intense search for him, myself, and the life energy I call God. It was not a thirty-day course with a step-by-step process. I couldn't put it in neat little categories. I know because I spent a lot of time trying.

I could only pick up my pen and journal. My pen drew a medium black line from point A (what I knew) to point B (something nearby that seemed similar) – a gathering of scattered bits of light, flickers of safety, connection, new life. I didn't understand this process. When I stopped to analyze it, I only spun in frustration. All I knew to do was gather up the tiny sparks of my past life and hope it would become more illuminating with time.

This was the way I stayed on Earth and did not permanently leave to find my son. As I put one anxious word in front of the other, the pen continued to tell me that I was writing towards greater light and understanding.

I wrote for a while, looking for those flashes and building a bit of courage to venture out for groceries. I bought necessary items at the familiar neighborhood store, then hurried home to write what I had just experienced.

As the pen showed me my successes and progress, I became braver. Its ink began connecting more familiar dots as they appeared: friends, events, places, and ideas. Each connection gave me strength, reminding me who I had been and what I was doing, describing who I am and what I am doing now. I put together this new foundation based on past knowledge and present experiences as I watched, listened, and wrote of my life.

This preface was to be the last piece I wrote for this book before a self-imposed deadline to finish by November 28, 2005. It would have been my son's thirtieth birthday. I scrambled, wanting to complete the journey. But the harder I tried to finish, the more unfinished I felt. I had so much yet to learn.

In August 2005 before going to Taos, New Mexico, for a writing workshop, I was diagnosed with breast cancer. I didn't understand. It was not in my family; I was not supposed to have breast cancer. But after a biopsy on a suspicious shadow that appeared on my yearly mammogram, the surgeon called to tell me it was a "favorable cancer." A favorable cancer? I heard that as an oxymoron. Then he offered me the choice of a lumpectomy with radiation therapy or a radical mastectomy.

"What's the difference?" I asked.

"Not much. It's just personal preference. One way is as effective as the other," he told me.

I felt like I was at Baskin-Robbins, choosing between pistachio almond and chocolate mint, and selected the lumpectomy only because he assured me I could postpone radiation until I got back from Taos. I also began taking Tamoxifen. Ah, the favorable part was becoming more apparent: there would be no chemotherapy.

The workshop in Taos was everything I wanted it to be. Twenty writers burning with stories to tell and eager to find a way to do it. We left New Mexico full of enthusiasm with plans to keep in touch.

But once I was back home I began six and one-half weeks of radiation treatments and soon discovered I hadn't dealt with the reality of this disease. Every day as I sat in a waiting room at the Cancer Treatment Center with patients in various stages of the illness, I was facing my own mortality. So much of my energy had been spent coming to terms with Carlton's death. It was now time to look at my own.

"Wait, God," I scribbled in my notebook, *"I'm not ready. I've still got a lot of stuff I want to do here. Oh? You're just checking? To see how serious I am? God, I am."*

The importance of my Taos connection became clearer. I stayed in touch with other writers as we shared weekly experiences and insights. The practice kept me focused and trusting that this was my way to greater understanding.

Then at the beginning of November, four weeks before my manuscript deadline, my mother and brother and I visited my ninety-year-old dad at the War Veterans Nursing Home in Monroe, Louisiana, a hundred miles away. He has Alzheimer's and we are never sure how coherent he will be when we visit, so Mother showed him family pictures hoping to help him connect to his own bits of light. This only seemed to frustrate him. He had a hard time completing sentences. While we sat in the day room with other men much like him, I listened to his struggle. Then I asked him what was going on. He talked about his mother and father and trying to get home.

"But they tell me not to come the regular way," he said. "Something's wrong with that, isn't it?"

"Your mother and dad are dead," I said.

He looked a bit surprised, then told me he was afraid the doctors would think he sounded crazy.

"No, Dad," I assured him. "You're just watching your home movies. The collection that makes up the unique story of Deane Flett."

He became calmer and more articulate. Before we left, I bent down to kiss him and he grabbed my hand. His pale blue eyes looked straight into my hazel ones.

"Thank you," he whispered.

It was a powerful link. I let Dad show me where he was and I understood it. It was his life in review. The same thing I was experiencing, as I wrote my way through this grief journey. I, too, was talking with the dead and reliving my past. I, too, often worried that I sounded crazy.

So now I must "finish" this book and let it go I know that even in published form, It's still not complete. It becomes, at best, a sharing of my experiences. This part of my journey offered as compassion for others looking for safety, or connection, or new life. I may not be in charge of anything more than that.

I poured out my heart as I worked to be as honest and thorough as I could. With much love, then, I release the book. It is much like my own son. It will go where it needs to go and connect with what it needs to connect.

I know now why I chose his birthday, the date that sometimes fell on Thanksgiving Day, as my deadline to complete this manuscript. I approached this year's designated-day-to-be-thankful and realized with tears in my eyes that November 28 will always be Thanksgiving Day for me.

The Princess and the journal

Darkness

The Phone Call

It was 9:30 at night on January 11, 2003, when the phone rang. Because I was so near sleep I didn't consider a call at that time of night might be bad news.

The next thing I knew "Kelly something" from Los Angeles County was asking me what my relation was to Carlton Harris.

"I'm his mother," I answered groggily.

"Well," she said, "I have some bad news."

Did I realize at this point that she was from the police department? Probably not.

She told me Carlton had been found dead.

What was she saying? Who was I talking to in this dark bedroom?

She told me again and a slight feeling stirred.

Then she wanted to know if there was a family history of medical problems.

I was trying to understand this noise on the phone.

"Does Carlton have a history of medical problems?"

"Oh, well, he has asthma, and he's had a couple of seizures," the mother of Carlton answered.

"Tell me about the seizures."

"There was one when he was quite young, fever-related. And then one a little later at the age of six or seven. He took phenobarbital for a year after that."

Why was "Carlton's mother" being asked about his health, I wondered. I wanted to be the one getting information, not the one giving it.

Kelly asked if there was a history of heart problems.

OK, that's enough. My assertive voice said, "Tell me what happened!"

She began some story about an e-mail he sent to a girl up north.

Up north? My logical mind sorted through this strange information. Where the hell was that?

"The girl was concerned and called the police. They broke into his apartment and found him."

At some point my sensible voice asked if this was a joke. I couldn't picture what she was telling me. Was this some TV show I fell asleep watching?

She told me it was not a joke and another vague feeling stirred.

"Was it suicide?" the voice from my mouth asked.

Kelly didn't know. There were no drugs or alcohol.

"Was there a note?"

"No."

"He attempted it once before about six or seven years ago." I felt further detached from this noise.

"Oh," Kelly said. And I wondered if they had even considered that.

"He's been running and he's a vegan," I said, in the voice of a mother proud of her son's lifestyle.

"A vegan?" she questioned.

What did that mean? I bristled, the tentative pride vanishing. Was Carlton missing some trace elements vital to his system? Did she have a problem with vegans? Or was this just a question?

"I don't know what I'm supposed to do," I whispered.

She said she would give me more information about that in a minute and continued her line of questioning. "Did he have a history of depression?"

"Well, yeah. It's sprinkled rather generously throughout our family," I said defensively.

"Was he taking anything?"

"Not that I know of." And this sad mother realized how little she did know about this man-child she birthed 27 years ago.

"The e-mail girl says he told her he was a sociophobe. Is that right?"

"It's very possible," I answered, wary of the droning voice of authority on the other end. I knew he called himself a severe introvert, which is also sprinkled generously throughout our family.

"What do I do now?" I asked quietly.

She told me his apartment had been sealed and my mind pictured duct tape and that yellow police line stuff. I felt like I was back in front of the TV.

Then she told me I needed to call a Los Angeles mortuary.

Really, I thought. I didn't happen to know of any.

Then she suggested calling one here in Shreveport and letting them call Los Angeles.

That sounded more doable, and that strange stirring inside me returned. My panicky voice offered an expletive and told her I was here by myself.

"Breathe," she said, "and call a friend when we finish talking."

My scared mind realized there were not a lot of people I felt comfortable calling. Leah was the obvious one. Linda's mother was in a hospice. And my brothers' band just started playing their first set at the Oak Creek Lounge.

Then there was talk about a medical examiner who would do an autopsy and might be able to tell us more.

Clutching my pillow, I asked how long he had been dead.

Kelly didn't know.

Man, those TV cops seem to be able to determine a lot more at the scene.

She gave me her name and number and told me she would be there until midnight. And then she would be back again on Wednesday. Because it was Saturday, I didn't hear that as helpful information.

She gave me a case number and hung up.

Did I understand what was happening? I felt like I was in a thick fog. I had no tears.

Who was this person holding the phone? Who were all these voices? Who was the person watching these scenes from a TV show? Who was I now?

Overwhelmed

I had no idea where I would find answers. But this feeling was strangely familiar.

I remembered being overwhelmed as I was nearing my 50th birthday in 1999. I just didn't realize it. I had been a public school teacher for nearly 30 years, beginning in the early days of court-ordered mass desegregation in the South. In March 1976, four months after the birth of our son Carlton, my husband left. For the next seven years I was a single parent with a full-time job, and Carlton became a daycare baby. I was responsible for birthday parties, homework and carpooling needs. I cooked fish sticks, baked beans, and corn on the cob, alternating days with

Happy Meals, and on the weekends the apartment got cleaned, or not. When Carlton was four, I bought a little house for the two of us, so we could have a backyard and a place of our own. When he was in first grade, I stayed up late making Valentine cupcakes for his class, writing every child's name in red icing across the top of the individual treats. My honest attempts at being a good mother. Then in 1983, I remarried and Carlton and I made room for another person in our lives. I was determined to make this union last.

I was an avid volunteer for every organization to which I belonged, taking jobs that no one else seemed to want. When I taught at a middle school, I was the yearbook sponsor. At the different churches where I held membership, I prepared lessons as a Sunday school teacher, sang in the choir and chaired the Worship Committee. I served in a soup kitchen and helped build houses with Habitat for Humanity. *I am woman; hear me roar.* And I was exhausted...

I had a beautiful loving son who was also eager to please. I miss his big kind eyes and sweet shy smile. He was tall, broad-shouldered, and very smart. He read voraciously and willingly accepted the challenges of calculus and physics. He left for college in the fall of 1994 with high hopes. His honest attempts at being a good son.

When Carlton left I thought I would have more time for myself and saw the empty nest as a welcomed change. When he came home from his less-than-successful freshman year, I worried he might want as much from me as I was giving my husband, job, and all my organizations, so we tried family counseling for a couple of months. But I felt too much of the burden. After each session my husband and son seemed to know their roles, and I continued responding as before. I stopped the sessions, thinking they might be the problem. Relief didn't come.

Then Carlton moved into his own apartment, holding part-time jobs and attending classes at the local college. It was there, in the spring of 1996, a friend found him unconscious. His first suicide attempt. Sleeping pills. Maybe he was exhausted, too. He moved back home.

Several months later my mother-in-law offered to pay for marriage counseling. My husband and I were both holding in a lot of emotion, and an objective counselor might help. So again we tried talk therapy. I spoke of frustrations and sadness. My husband sat quietly, expressing his feelings later at home. The therapist's office became the only place I felt safe, and again I felt too much of the burden. Something I was doing was obviously a problem. I didn't know how to communicate with my own husband, and he was rapidly becoming one of my biggest fears. I wanted to stop the counseling sessions and try a separation. By October of 1997, I knew I wanted a divorce and still needed help learning how to express myself honestly, so I began intense individual therapy with my minister.

Within months of my husband's moving out, Carlton set out on his own again, this time to the West Coast for a job he found on the Internet. I obviously didn't know how to talk to him, either, and all I could do was let him go with my blessing.

For a while I felt better living on my own and filled much of my time with teaching and volunteering. But at work there were additional assignments of bus duty and cafeteria monitoring, an abundance of local directives and documentation, and a national trend toward standardized curriculums. I was feeling overwhelmed again, even after letting go of the volunteer jobs no one else wanted. Maybe there were reasons others didn't want these jobs. I was tired of being a superwoman and people pleaser.

I had no idea where I would find answers. But the feeling was strangely familiar. "Who are you now?" I asked myself over and over again. There was that troubling question. "What is it that you want?"

Good mid-life crisis questions. No longer in therapy, I turned to my journal for solace, a safe place to talk honestly with myself. The pen reminded me of the parts of teaching I loved and gifts I wanted to share, but it also told me I needed to take care of myself. By the spring semester of 2001, I decided to retire. I wanted a scaled-down lifestyle with less outside interference. I was beginning to feel better again.

News from Carlton was nearly non-existent. After living in Eugene, Oregon, for a year-and-a-half, he moved with a friend to Hollywood, California, to set up a business installing and troubleshooting computer programs. When I did hear from him he sounded successful, so I let go of some of my spinning "mother worry." He seemed to have found a way to make use of his intelligence and make good money.

With pride he told me of a car he bought. He had a volunteer job with the Leukemia Foundation, became a vegan and was training for a marathon. But in the fall of 2002 he called to tell me he left his business friend and computer job, wanting something different. I assured him things would work out, like they were for me. His later calls became more vague, less about his job search and more about running, or movies, or the state of the nation. Maybe he was becoming overwhelmed again.

And I, busy finding a place that suited me, couldn't hear his distress. I wasn't as worried about homeland security and the nation on the brink of war, which I might have been concerned about earlier. I was finding serenity in letting go of things I have no control over. I was no longer trying to save the world. I was writing to save myself. Maybe I didn't realize then what I was doing. Maybe if I could have identified it, I could have been more help to Carlton. Maybe if I had encouraged him to try journaling, honestly conversing with himself, it would have saved him as well. Maybe if I had known better how to talk with my son. Maybe.

Now What?

In my dark bedroom after the call on January 11, 2003, and after dialing a phone number as Kelly told me, I heard Leah's voice. A current of reassurance ran through my numb body. I knew who I was when talking to Leah.

I was the retired teacher who volunteered weekly in Leah's kindergarten class at the school where I once taught science. I was also the scared five-year-old who needed a mother she could trust. So, of course Leah was the one to call. I watched her nurture scared five-year-olds all the time.

She left the party she was hosting for her son's baseball teammate, assuring me it was about over anyway. I didn't have the strength, or desire, to argue. Once here, she called my friend Linda, my brothers, and my former minister, even as I expressed concerns about bothering them. I had to trust she knew who this frightened child needed to connect with. She stayed overnight, with plans to leave in the morning for Sunday duties at her church. During the night I lay on my bed too afraid to close my eyes, too afraid to cry, too afraid to do much of anything, but I knew Leah, the nurturing mother, was in the next room. Now what?

Sometime in this dark, sleepless night, I wandered into my living room. Who was I now? I sat on the blue-flowered sofa, turned on the nearby table lamp, picked up my pen and black-and-white composition book. Another current of reassurance ran through me. I was the writer. The one who took up this very spot over two years ago when life was overwhelming, who left a successful teaching assignment, distancing herself from long-time friends, and who walked away from organizations that had once defined her.

In 1998, when my son left a practical job here with medical insurance and chances for advancement to follow his bliss on the West Coast, I began to want my own new adventure. I watched as my pen began carefully sorting through my life and uncovering deeply hidden dreams.

So on this cold winter's night I again turned to my pen.

There was the phone call. A Kelly something from Los Angeles. She asked about Carlton's medical history and told me about a girl up north. I'm supposed to call a mortuary. And Leah's asleep in the guest room.

In the morning, after Leah left, I was alone in this empty house. She would be back later with others. But for the moment I was on my own.

Breathe. I was again following the Kelly-voice's advice as I sat on my sofa.

One jarring phone call and everything was suspect. How could I ever trust again? All I knew to do was to grab two things I recognized — Leah, the friend outside myself, and my pen, the friend within — and this was where I began.

My grief journey. My grief journal. It seemed neither linear nor predictable as it began gathering pieces of my shattered life. It wrote me through an anxious afternoon when my overloaded emotions wanted to take over, and urged me to take care of the business at hand without letting feelings shut me down. It talked me out of the house and into the world to connect with what was once safe and familiar. Then when I'd had enough, it welcomed me back home to unleash the overwhelming anger and fear, away from others. It reported new behaviors I was testing and compared them to what I already knew. As I let go of this isolating safety to practice a more balanced conversation in my head, I found myself for longer periods of time in the world beyond my sofa.

But it wasn't until the second anniversary of Carlton's death, unsure how I would share this journey with others, that I began systematically reading the two dozen journals. I was blown away. I had been recording the process of my unfolding. Darkness, Reaching Out, Renewed Energy, God, A Path Through My Grief. It was the way I put together the pieces I now know as me. A collection of tiny sparks of light hiding in my shadows.

It took more than two years before I was far enough into this journey to identify where I had been, and another nine months before I was ready to share much of it. I now assume that was also part of the process.

In the Beginning

Where did this journaling obsession come from? For many years I taught language arts and really hated to teach writing. The emphasis for good writing was on grammar and structure, killing – or at least gravely wounding – any desire to tell an interesting story. And all those papers I wrote for graduate courses were pure agony, as I gathered research from an adequate variety of sources, footnoting everything, constantly monitoring for perceived plagiarism, and giving professors what I thought they wanted. I was learning the process of writing, but I had not yet heard my own voice.

I kept journals off and on during various stages of my life, as suggested by counselors and friends. I vowed to write daily, and kept the promise for about a month, or until I felt better, then discontinued the discipline until the next crisis urged me to pick up my pen again. The many attractively bound, partially filled journals all around the house are nevertheless informative, as they recorded where I was and provided practice for what was to come.

In February 1999, I gave a sermon at my church. It was a review of my spiritual journey at that time, as I was traveling deeper into my own therapy. That summer I presented a Blessing of the Animals service based on stories of my classroom pets. The preparation for each presentation connected events from my life in a form I could now see. Both services were well received and personally satisfying, so I continued to write classroom anecdotes as the 1999-2000 school year began.

Then, in December, my beloved minister and counselor resigned amid accusations of sexual misconduct. I felt confused and abandoned. I had had such strong feelings for him. I was the Worship Chair, so I held tightly to the organization, wanting to continue his ministry. But I soon found unfinished grief in that setting. When I spoke of my frustrations and sadness to others, I felt dismissed, adding to my fear. I didn't know how to make myself understood, so I quit talking about it. Five-and-a-half months of filling the pulpit with guest speakers consumed much of my energy, so I tried once more in a setting specifically offered for grief counseling. I felt confusion rapidly accelerating into anger. I was, after all, a volunteer with a full-time teaching job and a pen that wanted my attention. I lacked the stamina to continue the struggle. I needed to pull away and take care of myself.

That was when I began writing more than classroom stories. Discouraged by the response I received from outside sources, I began a second notebook for feedback from myself. I needed to learn how to com-municate more effectively, and initially the voice from my pen sounded a lot like my minister's. It was as if I were still listening to his wisdom on Sunday, or, as in therapy, being allowed to release my emotions in the safety of his office. It was the voice I missed, and the grief I sorely needed to heal. So I talked to my journal, my minister, my self. I wasn't sure who was doing all this talking. All I knew was that it was a vital connection.

My journal helped me make the choice to retire and explore this writing further, concentrating on the stories from my classroom. I thought the school anecdotes were what I needed to write about, and they were, for two-and-a-half years. Until the night of January 11, 2003, when I got a phone call from Los Angeles telling me my son was dead. I opened my notebook.

Gulp. Now what, God?

Hold on to your pen.

But this is new territory; I don't think I can make it.

Keep writing, sweetie. I'll talk you through it.

A Creative Response

In those first days following the call from California, I was all business. I needed to stay in control. Denial, shock, whatever, was calling on my school teacher persona to handle the overwhelming chaos swirling around me.

I decided there would be a service for the family on Saturday, and friends could visit at my house on Sunday afternoon. The Sunday plans easily took shape, as I willingly allowed Leah and my teacher friends to help with the details.

But the Saturday service I wanted to take on myself. Matt – my ex-husband and Carlton's adoptive father – his family, and my own frayed family, their ex's, and children hovered in the air, broken strands just beyond my grasp. I wanted us to sit together in the same room and face each other for Carlton's sake. I was feeling responsible for his death because I couldn't fix all of these chaotic relationships.

First, I went to my notebook to stop the pacing and endless circling around the room. The black ink on the white page was something to focus on and brought me back to the present. With this self-centering I could now plan the service. That's when I remembered the box of notecards Leah gave me for Christmas. They read, "I believe we are here for a reason. As each day unfolds, we see less of the shadow and more of the sun." It was a thought I was desperately clinging to, so I decided to use the cards as invitations for all who were part of Carlton's earthly family to share in a celebration of his life. With renewed energy, I drove around the city to hand-deliver the local ones.

A couple days later, Matt's sister called saying she and her mom were coming from Austin. Her voice sounded so engaging. Why did I feel unbalanced, as if I was about to be side-swiped? I had always enjoyed being with her, but the last time we were together was with her parents in Boston in the summer of 1996. That was after Carlton's year at college, the less-than-successful family counseling and Carlton's first attempt at suicide, and before the year-long marriage counseling, messy divorce and Carlton's sudden move to the West Coast. At that time in Boston we talked around the troubling events. Matt, her older brother, had struggled with self-concept issues and his own suicide attempt as a young adult. I was hoping to find relief being with a family who had experienced this challenge, but all I could do was cry. I had no words to express myself, and the other vacationers stayed busy with other things. Then in 1999, I talked to her on the phone and shared a troubling concern I had about Matt's erratic behavior. Again I hoped we might connect, but it didn't happen the way I expected. Now I didn't know what to expect.

As I was thinking of this sister-in-law, another one called, angry because a certain ex-wife would be there. I listened to her frustration and understood her discomfort, but I had no answers. All I did was issue invitations, and now I felt scared. I needed to talk to my notebook now.

What have I initiated?

A gathering of Carlton's family.

But there'll be chaos. We've all been
holding an awful lot in.

*What was your intention in getting
everyone together?*

To be in the same room so we could
look at each other.

*Then that's what will happen.
Watch everything. Listen to what
is said. We can talk about it later.*

A gold-framed picture of Carlton running a half-marathon in November was surrounded by little tea candles, gifts from one brother's wife, set up on the antique coffee table, a past Christmas present from my other brother. Two potted blooming azalea bushes, one from Matt's parents and one from cousins, added color to the living room. The house sparkled because my teacher friends paid to have it cleaned for the occasion. Platters of food filled the dining room table, and the essence of a spicy taco soup made by an ex-sister-in-law wafted from the kitchen. In the background the ethereal sounds of Charlotte Church's *Voice of an Angel* CD played. And, of course, the proverbial "elephants" lingered everywhere. This was, after all, the living room.

There were awkward attempts at connecting, as Carlton's family converged at the house where Carlton spent nine years of his abbreviated life. When I opened the front door to Matt's mother and sister, I received warm hugs. But when I moved to Matt, he felt like stone, and I quickly pulled back, registering this feeling for the later conversation with my notebook.

Matt, supported by his mother and sister, stayed near the entrance. Bruce and Buddy, my brothers, were present, as were two of their ex-wives, one current wife, and a teen-aged daughter. I, too, was grateful for family support in this uncomfortable setting. My aging mother and father were also there, but I was unable to assess how they were holding up. Dad wanted to know if sharing an experience about Carlton as a child was appropriate. I assured him it was. Mother wanted the music turned off; I turned it down.

As we took seats around the coffee table. I felt everyone was watching me, so I worked to stay detached and stoic. Was this the legacy of my Midwestern ancestry, the knowledge of a nearby comforting notebook, the grace of shock, or a little of it all? I took a deep breath and began the celebration by thanking everyone for coming. I read Emily's speech from the third act of *Our Town*, the play I had been in the month before. Then I shared two stories I had written, one from my science classroom about the death of an iguana and one recently written for my friend Linda, whose mother was in a hospice.

As I lit one of the small candles to the memory of Carlton, I invited others to share. One by one a diversity of gifts was presented: a poem read by his maternal grandmother, a picture with his cousin Caleb at their grandparents' lake house, and a Bible verse shared by Matt, the preacher's son.

My father recalled sitting with a young Carlton in the church balcony, where he once sat with his own children. Carlton's Aunt Lydia remembered the large collection of G. I. Joes he gave Caleb. Recent news of Carlton came from his outgoing Uncle Buddy who had been in touch with Carlton's friends in California. From his Uncle Bruce came a sad reminiscence of sharing the same birthday.

One by one each person presented a connection, then lit a candle. Avery, Carlton's oldest Flett cousin and now the oldest Flett grandchild, also lit candles for her little half-brother and sister and their mom, who were not present. Matt's mom lit a candle for Matt's dad, who was also not there. I mentally recorded the illumination from the collection of tiny candles as I watched, detached, sitting on the sofa, gathering images and feelings from the afternoon. I listened as words, said and unsaid, vibrated through the living room.

The solemn service ended with the nourishing communion of food and more relaxed conversation of other news. I had provided the opportunity to come together. It was all I could be responsible for before each of us left to begin our own grief journey.

Safety

A Safe Place

My first real trip away from the safety of my house was to a friend's home after school on the Friday before the weekend memorial service and visitation. Our regular meeting of active and retired Stoner Hill Elementary teachers was located in a noisy Mexican restaurant where we, the soon-to-be-dubbed "Steel Magnolias," unwound from the week, compared notes, shared funny stories, and bitched. These were the friends who organized the Sunday visit.

Martha decided her house would allow us more privacy for our Friday meeting after Carlton's death. Leah was there, as were several others who had stopped by or called through the week, but Martha's gathering was the first time I met the whole group together. Her dining table was loaded with party food and plenty of champagne-laced orange juice mimosas. At first I didn't want a drink, but when my friends emphasized my need for vitamin C, I submitted. I found making conversation stressful, even with these well-meaning friends, and was grateful for the drink. It allowed me to be present without needing to participate.

By the next Friday, after the challenge of the memorial service and visitation for me, and a busy school week for my friends, we met back at our restaurant's big round table, picking up our routine. I don't know what we talked about, or if I even talked that day; I just remember hearing noise. But I was glad to see myself out and about. Any real conversation was saved for later, in the safety of my home and notebook.

People are advised to get back to a regular routine as soon as they can after experiencing the trauma of grief. My regular routine, however, consisted of sitting on the sofa pushing a pen. I allowed few outside distractions, and now realized how heavily I relied on words appearing in the notebook to tell me who I was.

The weekly meeting with my friends was one event beyond my living room I could count as routine. It was now more than a gathering to compare school stories or surface situations. I was not yet ready to share scarier feelings, leaving those for my notebook. But my life had been turned upside down, and I needed a safe place to land. I found it in the laps of middle-aged public school teachers, most with grown children of their own, eager to do what they knew best — mother.

I didn't have school stories to tell. These friends couldn't relate to my writing obsession. They wanted to share news of their children. It wasn't always easy being a part of the group. Sometimes I felt incredibly empty. Sometimes I was filled with fear. I was no longer a teacher. No longer a mother. I was not a published writer. But week after week, I kept showing up to sit in this circle of friends, to remind myself that I, too, was a strong Southern woman.

I am grateful to these women who continued working to find common ground and to explore our friendships' more challenging levels. We have shared joys and concerns of grandbabies, awards, weddings, retirements, trips, illnesses, funerals, and birthdays. Our weekly conversations ranged from dealing with difficult peers and aging parents to finding a good plumber and arguing with insurance companies. We were a circle of friends who wanted to connect.

Some teachers moved on and others took their place. Some didn't come often, but knew they were welcome when they did. Some of us were more "steel;" some more "magnolia." But our round table continued to offer a safe place and an invitation to come as you need to be.

Avery

The one person to get any extended attention from me in the first few weeks after Carlton's death was Avery, my popular high-school niece, who was struggling in accelerated classes.

Earlier, I had discussed with my brother Bruce, Avery's dad, the possibility of tutoring her. I requested there be no money paid during the trial period, in case I wasn't Avery's solution. By the end of January we decided to proceed with the plan. I wanted to be with the other children in my family and remember what I once knew how to do.

Avery came over with a set of heavy textbooks issued for home use to leave in my living room, and we went straight to work. I was eager to explore our relationship, as I had never had much time alone with this strawberry-blond beauty. She is the outgoing grandchild of the family. Carlton was much more reserved and studious, as are Avery's half-siblings, Jake and Laura Beth. At first she followed my academic lead with enthusiasm. We sat on the living room sofa reading history and discussing South American revolutions. *Antigone*, her English assignment, got translated into a more modern lingo. She seemed to know how to play the game in biology and French, and we were both intimidated by geometry. By mid-nine weeks her grades went up, with an A in history and a passing grade in English.

Although Avery was trying hard to please me, I knew she was also growing weary reading textbooks and studying for tests with her Aunt Laura. I watched as she began to pull away. The initial three or four nights a week together became one or two. She told me of study groups she found with her friends. This was the motivation we wanted, but I was ambivalent about losing the contact. I looked forward to our time together and her willingness to connect.

So I took my concerns to the notebook, not wanting to burden her with my needs. I found ways to honestly

Laura with niece Avery.

commend her for trying her own solutions. The original plan was just to explore possibilities. She was learning what it took to pass enriched classes, and I was learning not all teenagers were interested in them.

Did I make her an A student? No, that didn't seem to be what she wanted. Had this been my goal? I hope not, but I spent many journal pages relinquishing that plan.

I was, however, learning so much more than I had imagined, as Avery and I shared intimate stories of our family. She, the big sister, told of concerns for her younger siblings, and I related my own about her dad and uncle, my younger brothers. We discussed feelings about suicide and death. One of her friend's sisters died this way a few months before Carlton. We both needed to talk. And we compared notes on my aging parents, her grandparents. We had so much in common.

By March, Avery and I went our separate ways, although her textbooks remained in my living room until the end of the semester. She had obviously found another way to finish up the year. I remembered how little I was able to "help" Carlton with his schoolwork at this age. Maybe it's one way an adolescent pulls away to become more independent.

On St. Patrick's Day I went with a friend to hear my brothers' band play at an outdoor city festival. Avery was there with friends, in all their teen-aged radiance, and we danced together to the family's music. First I imitated her modern moves, then she mirrored mine from the '60s. It was now this outgoing woman-child's turn to tutor her timid aunt in the art of being festive.

The Dream

In the first few months, on my scariest nights I would hold on to the brass headboard of my bed, afraid of being swallowed by the darkness. Was this the darkness Carlton gave in to? The thought made me grip the cold metal tighter.

But in the middle of May, about four months after his death, I had a dream. I remembered no images, only sounds. I was to pick up my son and a friend from a church activity, but Carlton called in a somewhat raspier version of his voice, "Mom, here's the deal. I want to stay tonight. The team is playing and we missed the last game. I can get my medallion some other time."

I awakened suddenly, looking around the dark bedroom for the familiar voice, frantic to know what it meant. He loved baseball. Had he found the perfect team? Was "missing the last game" a reference to his first suicide attempt? Was it important for me to know he had chosen to spend the night at church? The voice in my head was asking too many questions.

Then there was mention of a medallion. What was that about? Was he given the impossible role of family hero, the only child of a first-born mother and an only-child father? The first grandchild on either side. By the time he was four months old, his father and I separated and Carlton had little contact with him. What did I do wrong? What should I have done differently? When he was seven years old I remarried and he was adopted by my second husband, Matt, who was also the first-born of his family. Carlton then became the first grandchild for Matt's family. There were so many expectations riding on those broad shoulders of his. What should I have realized earlier? How could I have known? And he said he can get his medallion some other time. What in the world did that mean?

I grabbed my pen and notebook. I needed something wiser than this questioning voice in my head to talk me through these mounting fears.

What did I do to my precious son?

You only did what you knew. Generations of family experiences and birth-order responsibilities as you understood them.

But I've made so many mistakes. How do I go on? What do I do now?

Well, tell me what you have been doing.

I gave a family memorial service for Carlton. A chance to come together privately, away from the well-meaning public and friends.

That's good, what else?

Well, then I pulled away from my immediate family.

That's OK.

I didn't have the energy to take care of anyone but me.

I said that's OK.

I tutored Avery. There were lunches with my brother Buddy at George's Grill. I babysat Jake and Laura Beth.

All very good.

That was easy. I knew how to do those things. But the rest of my family...

What about them?

Well, Buddy brought my daddy by on Valentine's Day to give me a rose. I remember holding tightly to him in my driveway. I felt like a little girl.

That makes sense.

But I can only talk to brother Bruce through e-mails. He seems so overwhelmed. And I'm avoiding Mother altogether. I'm afraid they'll take too much energy.

That's OK for now. You're doing the best you can. They'll understand. Things will change when they need to.

I'm volunteering in Leah's classroom again. I know how to help there. And meeting my teacher friends on Fridays feels comfortable enough. But some of the friends I haven't been in touch with lately scare me, and I'm not sure why.

Don't push yourself if you're not ready. You'll understand when it's time.

I meet with my writing group every Sunday afternoon. I know how to participate there.

It sounds like you're doing just what you need to do.

Really?

Sure. Just do the best you can and keep talking to me.

And who was I these first months of darkness? I was still the daughter, the sister, the aunt, the mother, the teacher, the friend, and the writer. And in time, as I felt ready to step back into the light that is life on Earth, I found new ways to know who I am and where I belong. I just kept talking to my notebook.

Ashes

A soft voice on the other end of the line told me the package containing my son's remains had finally come from a crematorium in California and I could come pick it up at the local funeral home. I went that afternoon.

But when I got home I put the unopened package on the table next to his framed marathon picture. That was enough courage for one day. Something didn't make sense. The picture and the package couldn't be the same person. For days all I did was walk by the table and assess my strength. I couldn't do this by myself; I needed help from my pen.

I can't open the box. I'm too scared.

That's OK, sweetie.

But it needs to be taken care of. I need to move on.

Relax, Laura. You'll know when you're ready.

So I continued to scribble in my notebook, and several days later I found myself opening the package. Inside was a brown plastic rectangular box, not the imagined burial urn. Nothing good enough to hold my beautiful son. I took some deep breaths, then unsnapped the plastic box, untwisted the tie on the plastic bag and touched the light gray powder. This can't be Carlton. Twenty-seven years of flesh and blood could not be so easily reduced to an ash-filled baggie. I found official papers from the crematorium tucked inside the fine dust, and little lumps of bone, and oh, dear, a string and metal tag etched with his name. A toe tag. My mind traveled to images from the movies, then back to the reality of my living room. *Breathe*, I told myself.

For several days I just practiced opening the box, looking at its contents, touching it, and wondering if I would ever be able to let it go.

My plan was to scatter Carlton's ashes on the Caddo Lake Nature Trail, where I had gone just two days before his death, desperately seeking my own peace. On that troubling day, within minutes of feeling the firm footing beneath me and inhaling the fresh air all around, I had found overwhelming connection. A tingling sensation ran through my body and warmth surrounded me. I was a completed circuit. As I continued walking, allowing balance to settle back into me, I came upon a clearing. A dozen tiny songbirds — nuthatches, chickadees, and finches — flew through with much rejoicing. Yes, I thought later, replaying the amazing scene over and over in my head. That was where my son, once the head chorister for the Shreveport Boychoir, would find rest.

It took several weeks and much journaling before I could separate the gray ash in the brown plastic box from my image of Carlton. I chose to go to the Texas state park alone, afraid of the energy I might need if anyone else was with me. The 45-minute drive gave my spinning mind time to let go of any last-minute doubts. At the entrance I told the park ranger I wouldn't be there long, and she waived the $2 day fee. I claimed this as assurance that I was right where I was supposed to be and drove down the steep park road to the trail's parking lot, turned off the engine, climbed out of the car with the box, and hiked to the place where the songbirds flew.

Once there I stood on the path, looking into the sunlit clearing, deeply breathing in the fresh air, and steadying my shaking hands. Then I unsnapped the box and took out a handful of ash. This was hard. My heart was pounding. The act of physically letting go was different from the release of spinning thoughts. Tears streamed down my face as I tossed one tentative fistful after another and watched the powder drift through the air and land among bamboo, decomposing leaves, and dirt trail. But halfway through the task I had stopped crying. The tingling and warmth returned, and the event felt incredibly powerful. I was now slinging the dust higher and letting it scatter farther, as if in celebration.

When the box was empty, I turned my attention away from where the ashes had fallen to the other side of the trail. There was a tree stump covered in resurrection fern, another sign for me that this truly was a place of profound connection. Mother Nature — the perfect setting for my child to find rest.

Raising a Princess

Princess, a scruffy, white and apricot terrier poodle, lies sprawled in a comfortable puddle on my lap while I write. She's my puppy alter ego.

By the time the little dog was four years old, we had each settled into a routine, our boundaries more or less defined. But the first two years were a struggle. I forgot how much constant attention a puppy demands, as I battled a personality as stubborn as my own. Her annoying chewing and yapping were a continuous challenge. Housebreaking the pup made Carlton's toilet training seem easy, and she was as hard to bathe and groom as that wiggly boy once was. Some battles I won; some I learned to give in to, calling them a truce of sorts. She goes outside to pee now, but her stuffed Beanie Baby toys are strewn all over the house.

Although still much like a small child, she has been very good company on this difficult journey. Princess is so tuned to my moods I wonder how she reads my mind. If I feel closed-in and antsy, the fluffy dog stands on her hind legs and whines for a walk. If I am lonely and at loose ends, she jumps into my lap. When her rough pink tongue begins licking my face, my first impulse is to push her away. But if I hesitate for a moment and allow the affection, I realize it's what I really wanted.

I pushed Carlton away, too. After a full day of teaching fifth graders, I'd pick him up at daycare and we'd head home where I'd immediately collapse on the sofa. He would then climb into my lap, ready for attention. A setting much like my times with Princess. I didn't have enough energy for the busy little guy. I couldn't see his needs; I was so overwhelmed by my own. A current of anxiety ran through my body as I wrote this, reminding me of another feeling I once had.

On the Saturday morning I believe Carlton was conceived, there was warmth in my womb. It was a stirring, but not an anxiousness. More like an assurance. I knew I was pregnant six weeks before a doctor's verification and before home tests were available. His father wasn't pleased and wanted little to do with this growing presence. I had used a foam contraceptive, I reasoned, having been the one responsible for birth control. We were not planning to start a family. But I couldn't let this new feeling go; I felt him stir.

I also remember having painful cramps late one night when I was six months pregnant. Afraid of what they could mean, I spent a long time alone in our tiny bathroom, crying and bargaining with God for a healthy baby. Three months later seven-pound, fifteen-ounce Carlton arrived.

Princess is another assurance, another chance. It's not an inner stirring this time. She's the frisky outer puppy inviting my inner puppy to come out and play. She chases squirrels through the backyard and barks at the neighborhood cats, who sit calmly watching her tirade from the top of the cinderblock fence. I wonder with chagrin if I'm that stubborn about things I have no control over.

Princess takes naps, lying draped over the top of the sofa or completely relaxed on her back in the middle of the living room, her pink tummy exposed. So trusting of her surroundings. I envy that.

It takes effort to balance both my notebook and an eight-pound dog in my lap when I want to write. These task-driven times trigger my impatience. Yet when I stare at the blank page, clueless what to do next, her attention offers a solution. Do I tell her enough how important she is?

Carl Jung said the creation of something new is not accomplished by the intellect, but by the play instinct acting from inner necessity. The creative mind plays with the objects it loves.

As my mind jumps around looking for impossible answers for past regrets, the scruffy princess encourages my creative energy, urging me to let go and participate, and reminding me of my own royal opportunities.

My Living Room

Most of my journaling takes place on a hide-a-bed sofa in the middle of the living room. Sitting here picking at pink and blue threads on the back cushion as I wait for formless thoughts to take shape, I imagine how this material was made. Overhead there are two large rectangular skylights, added soon after moving in, when we realized how dark this room was, even in the middle of the day. When I stretch out on this book-and-paper cluttered sofa with the fluffy dog on my lap and a Mary Englebreit woven throw covering my feet, I can watch clouds and birds pass above me.

Stacks of ongoing projects in this room make it a mess, something I would have worried about once upon a time. Now I just shrug it off as my natural state, knowing that when things get too messy even for me, I'll have a spontaneous burst of cleaning-frenzy energy and begin stirring things up.

Large watercolor paintings by two local artists hang on the walls. There are prints of school children in classrooms, flowers and birds, a Habitat for Humanity poster and one on childhood hunger. Images reminding me who I have been. A dozen silver- and gold-framed pictures of children sit on my small roll-top secretary. It is as if Carlton, my nieces and nephew, special children from school or church, and the child of a dear young teacher-friend are poised nearby to "watch" as I write.

Two bookcases are crammed with a diverse mix of books on the subjects of education, women's issues, politics, nature, and spirituality. Some were signed by the authors when I, eager to be in the company of writers, attended their lecture or workshop. There are also some favorite children's books, both from my childhood and classroom.

My maternal grandmother's anniversary clock sits to the right of the sofa on a side table that was also hers. My grandparents bought it in the '30s. It isn't presently working. Perhaps our connection does not run on Earth time. Her corner hutch near the skylight displays crystal goblets ringed with silver, presents from my 1974 wedding. On one shelf are pictures of my grandmother and Carlton, each as young children, along with two angel figurines. They shared the birth date of November 28.

Carlton's Raggedy Andy doll sits in a small wooden student chair just under the side table. Another "child" watching me. A table and chairs bought from a friend for a bargain price fill the dining area of the room. Two of the nicer pieces in here, an oversized dark blue upholstered chair and stained-glass buffet, were obtained at another friend's garage sale. In one corner, a threadbare rocking chair with a pinned-on lace doily covering one of the more obvious worn spots accumulates stacks of books and papers. This rocker is identical to the one in which my dad spent much time in the den of our family home.

On top of the larger bookcase a light blue ceramic parakeet, three painted wooden birds, a tiny brass owl, and a pair of brown clay doves perch among an assortment of birdhouses. My maternal grandfather's field glasses anchor one corner. Perhaps, because I often say God speaks to me through birds, it seems logical to have them above my writing space ready to impart their special messages.

But there's something else in this room that may go unseen to the casual observer. Conversations of family and friends continue to vibrate in the air. And there are faint images from this setting's past. I can see Carlton on the edge of the rocking chair playing Nintendo for hours — his beginning fascination with computers. Did I notice then how intensely he worked at manipulating the data on a baseball game, allowing him to design his perfect team? My dad, in his own rocking chair, would watch baseball games on television with the same intensity. He was part of a partnership obtaining the first television station license for Shreveport in 1953.

Many evenings this dining table waited, spread for the family meal. But anger and sadness from comments or facial expressions challenged any illusion I might have had of a Norman Rockwell setting. I wanted to recreate the stimulating dinner conversations I remembered as a child. Perhaps I did. The table now holds a clutter of papers and books.

The memorial service with Carlton's family plays through the air, reminding me of our coming together. I can see where everyone sat and hear what we said, each trying in our own way to connect. Here on the sofa Avery and I studied history as we learned of each other. I was discovering common ground and becoming less attached to my idea of how things should be. And this is where I continue to talk intimately to my notebook, gaining confidence to be a participant beyond these walls again.

There are so many kind words, angry words, sad words, and unspoken words swirling around in here. Sorting through all this noise can easily overwhelm and agitate me when I try to grab hold of it. But warm sunbeams shine through the windows in my ceiling, cutting into the chaotic sound waves, brightening the room, and beckoning me to let go and look up. I watch the drifting cloud wisps and soaring birds, and my rapid, shallow breathing and racing, jumbled thoughts slow down. A sense of calm works its way through my anxiety. I pick up my pen and notebook, ready again to see the words from within.

Walks in the Park

Princess jumped up and down the sofa and whined while I wrote in my notebook.

"Do you want a walk or something?" I asked impatiently, and she headed for the kitchen door.

Now I had no choice; I made the mistake of asking. To ignore her would bring more whining, and I wasn't sure how much more I could tolerate. The weather had been cool and damp for several weeks as winter in Shreveport wound down, so I had postponed our daily walks. But the day was brisk and we were between showers when I drove to a nearby city park to walk the all-weather path around tall trees and an algaed creek. I pulled into the parking lot and opened the car door. The fresh pine smell took me back to the Girl Scout camp I loved as a child. Maybe the frisky dog's idea for a walk was a good one.

My writing life craves daily walks. The sedentary schedule of sitting on a sofa all day was quite a change from keeping up with twenty-five active children in a classroom. My body wanted more stimulation.

Most mornings I begin with a solitary hike in the park near the Red River, circling through grassy wetlands on the concrete road, when it is not underwater after a particularly rainy season. Water birds get their breakfast of crawfish, bugs, and small fish before they start their day, and the sights and sounds of a morning routine inspire me. There have been some regular walkers here — a friendly woman and her big black lab, Lucy; a timid man with earphones and a hurried gait; and several runners. We acknowledge each other with our standard ritual of a smile or small talk as we pass.

Another trail, through more manicured gardens behind an art gallery, is good for hikes later in the day with a small, scruffy dog, except during the height of azalea and dogwood season. Then, every bride and Easter-dressed child stand posed beside the brightly colored spring flowers. My friendly Princess is all too eager to take her place in their picture.

Sometimes my morning walks take me to the track at the elementary school I attended as a child, while students arrive on campus. Or, later in the morning, to the park down the street from the first little house Carlton and I called our own.

Each location fills a different need. Sometimes I walk to be on a schedule, for my former teacher self. Sometimes a walk offers material to test my observation skills, or helps me break from a cycle of anxious, spinning thoughts. But often it is just a calming assurance that there's a grander plan than any I could imagine between the walls of my living room. Something deeper, something I couldn't quite identify, but something that might become clearer in time.

I watch one season transform into another and listen for rebirth within myself. Staying present during this daily journey moves me through past fears and away from future concerns. And the day a flock of tiny bluebirds flew out of a tree I passed, I remembered this is the magical walk called life.

Carlton's Stuff

Michael, Carlton's friend in California, called to offer help, sparing me the overwhelming task of vacating his apartment. I was grateful. I did not want to go to California at that time. Michael notified friends and business associates of Carlton's death, distributed clothing and furniture to local charities, then packed up his books, tapes, and movies to ship to me. He also sent Carlton's powerful computer.

Within days of our phone conversation, eight big boxes arrived. The young UPS guy was eager to chat with me about receiving such a mother lode until I told him they were from my son, who had died. He quickly departed. The boxes sat stacked in the middle of my narrow kitchen, which was as far into the house as the delivery man had permission to set them. Over the next few days I moved them one by one to Carlton's old bedroom.

One box was much lighter than the others. I opened this one first, thinking there might be something inside I should take care of. It contained correspondence, bills, and tax records, and it was overwhelming. I had no idea where to begin and hurried out of the room just to catch my breath. The next day my brother's lawyer friend told me not to worry about sorting through it; just wait a while. So I practiced waiting, turning to my notebook when I couldn't do it by myself. A couple months later when a creditor called asking for Carlton, I told him he had died. The creditor put me on hold to listen to the Carpenters sing "Close to You" while he checked the computerized public records. Returning several minutes later he notified me that "Carlton" was now released from any outstanding debt. I felt my own release. That was all the permission I needed to bag up the shoeboxes of papers and envelopes and carry them to the curb on trash day. That part was over.

Another box was packed with audiovisual materials. Avery eagerly claimed the DVDs one night during tutoring since I didn't have a DVD player. *The Lion in Winter* and *Pretty Woman* are movies the cousins now share. I picked through his assortment of videos, audiotapes, and CDs, recognizing some as part of the collection I had heard drifting from his bedroom at night before he left Shreveport. There was a diverse mix of movies and music, and I smiled when I found some that I also own. Digging through the titles I imagined what was going on inside him when he had watched and listened to this assortment. I held on to the ones that interested me and took the others in a big box to Mother's house for the rest of the family to go through. As far as I know, they are still over there in the box, untouched.

The other boxes were heavy with the weight and smell of books. Carlton, like me, was an avid reader.

Included were science fiction, Kurt Vonnegut, and John Irving. I recognized some from discussions we had during phone conversations. Some might have been assigned reading from past college classes. Others didn't seem to make much sense. Maybe they were book club selections, sent automatically when the monthly order form wasn't returned on time. At least that's how I accumulated some of my own collection. I was trying so hard to figure his life out. What did these books tell him? How did he connect?

I repacked several boxes for a local book bazaar, took a Bible and book of poetry to Mother, and kept a box for myself. In time, Uncle Buddy got the baseball books.

Movies, music, books — these were interests my family shared and expressions I could relate to.

Then, a few weeks later, the computer arrived. It was packed in three big boxes, left just inside my living room near the front door by a different UPS guy, again for me to carry box by box back to his bedroom. I couldn't open it. According to Michael, it was an impressive state-of-the-art computer, and my own little laptop was rather limited. But it was too much a part of the Carlton I didn't know. It was his passion and obsession, and it scared me. It was something I couldn't connect with, so it loomed still securely packaged in the middle of his old bedroom.

One evening when my friend Linda and I went out for supper, she mentioned her computer had crashed.

She was teaching education courses at a local college, and a working computer was essential. I immediately thought of the unopened boxes and offered her Carlton's computer. At first she took it as a loan, in case I might want it back someday, but after a month when I still had no interest in it, I knew it was for Linda, whom I claim as my "big sister," and I let her buy it from me. She knew Carlton as a baby. We met at a church singles program after I moved back to Shreveport in 1976. Her two daughters, collectively called "GinaCindy" by Carlton, sat with him in church while Linda and I sang in the choir together. This part of Carlton will be safe with Aunt Linda.

Bit by bit I dispensed of my son's belongings, hoping to know him better as I handled his possessions. He offered such a diverse set of clues. But I knew I was not really learning about Carlton. He was not a collection of things. I have been learning about myself in his life. One box at a time.

Caged Birds

A female albino ring-necked dove perches in a cage on my sunroom's tiled floor. The bird is the last remaining animal from the science class I taught at Stoner Hill Elementary School. She was the mother of six babies who hatched, were fed, and learned to fly in the presence of many junior naturalists. The father bird died, after conscientiously doing his duty, sitting on eggs, feeding babies, and giving flying lessons. It was an equal partnership. The babies have since been given away, have flown away, or have died, so now the caged mother is left alone in my sunroom to sing her mourning song and occasionally break into a sound resembling laughter. I understood her sad tune, but what triggered that joyful sound? Did she remember the thrill of seeing her children learn to fly? Was she recalling a funny story from our class?

Several years ago there was a rather noisy, messy pair of light blue parakeets sharing this sunroom with her. They were also in my classroom for a while, until I realized we didn't need any more noise or mess. They left school earlier than the rest of us.

In June 2001, less than a month after my retirement, the Flett family reunion gathered in my backyard for a crawfish boil. It was the last time Carlton was in Shreveport and the first time he met most of my dad's side of the family.

My niece, Laura Beth, left the parakeets' cage door open after trying to pet them. The in-and-out traffic through the sunroom door was too much temptation for the adventurous girl bird. Out she flew, leaving her mate behind.

On the last day of the reunion, after taking Carlton to the airport, two cousins and I were sitting in the quiet of my house when we noticed how lonely the little boy bird seemed. He was used to following the antics of his more active partner. We decided he too should be set free, if that's what he wanted, so I unhinged the cage, opened the sunroom door, and out he flew. Within minutes of his escape, we heard what had to be two parakeets answering each other somewhere high in the neighbors' trees. Was this the joy of flying free?

Eighteen months later, after Carlton died, I received many cards from his friends and business acquaintances in California because his friend Michael had given them my address. One was from a woman telling of her friendship with Carlton over the Internet, sharing their depressive tendencies and how they worked around them. I was relieved to know he had someone to talk to.

She said she and Carlton shared a favorite movie, *The Shawshank Redemption*, and quoted from the movie about how some birds are not to be caged and when they are released there is a rejoicing, even as we miss them.

Carlton must have known the loneliness of being a caged bird wanting release. I see the lonely boy parakeet on the day I took him to the airport. The last time I saw him. I can't catch my breath. Maybe he was feeling like a caged bird. I'll keep scribbling.

Ah, but his scattered ashes lie on the path of songbirds. Perhaps he's truly flying free.

I listened to the song of my dove in the next room, as I sat on the sofa scribbling to connect these thoughts. I was the caged mother bird mourning her child, laughing occasionally at memories, and writing for my own release.

Reaching Out

Reentry

Often I had overwhelming fears I would never return to a normal life. Before Carlton died, I'm not sure how "normal" I was, sitting on a sofa all day writing about teaching experiences. Afterward I wondered what normal was supposed to be for me. Maybe being aware of my life, learning from the past, watching the present and visualizing a future was the best I could hope for. I didn't really want to be as removed from the world as I had been, but I wondered if I would ever feel safe enough to reenter the fray. Could I let go of these paralyzing fears long enough to participate in a more active life again?

One morning I sat and wrote until I got antsy, then took a brisk walk in the neighborhood park with Princess. When I came home to try writing again that restless feeling returned. I wanted to be "doing" something else, so I consulted my rather short list of safe things to do.

Surely there is something I need at the grocery store. A trip through cereal aisles and frozen-food displays doesn't seem very exciting. Maybe I could sit in the sunroom and type my stories into the computer.

I got off the sofa and turned on my computer to begin tapping in new work. But the pokey computer was too slow to react, making me impatient. I knew I didn't want any more anxiety.

It's nearly noon. Too early to take a nap. What else can I try? I could get some lunch out, then go to the library to write.

I liked that idea, so I picked up my woven bag full of pens and notebooks and drove to the nearby barbeque restaurant. However, when I pulled in, I felt uneasy. The parking lot was nearly full. *Breathe,* I told myself, and pushed past the uneasiness so I would not automatically return home. I parked the car and went in. There was a long, loud line extending to the door. The crowd inside matched the abundance of cars outside. "*Breathe,* Laura," I repeated, inhaling the sweet, smoky air, and willing myself to stay. I could at least get a sandwich to go.

By concentrating on my breath while waiting in line, I found I was ready to stay and eat. I took my chopped beef sandwich and side order of cole slaw to a booth by the window and set my black-and-white notebook beside my plate in silent support. I watched the noisy crowd of people eating their lunches. They were making small talk with each other, while their eyes darted around the room. That was interesting. They didn't appear any more confident than I felt.

I finished my lunch with renewed energy and decided to drive to the nearby library branch. Pulling into its nearly-full parking lot without a second thought, I turned off the engine, pulled up the emergency brake between the front seats, and got my bag. I climbed out of the car, closed and locked the door, put my keys in my pocket, and took several steps toward the library. But I stopped, turned around, and walked back to the car to peek through the window and double-check the position of the brake. Satisfied by this compulsive little ritual, I headed toward the building with confidence, passed through the sliding doors and down the center of the busy modern media room to the floor-to-ceiling windows in the periodicals section. I dropped into a comfortable chair with a view of the duck pond, letting my bag fall to the floor. As I bent over to dig out a pen and notebook, the sunlight through the glass warmed my back. I was ready to write again, eager to "see" what I had been "doing."

> Here I am. One foot, or maybe one word, in front of the other.
>
> **You're doing great.**
>
> Why do I get so scared? Was Carlton's fear of people my fear of people?
>
> **I don't know. What do you think?**

Are there people in here worrying about the same thing? How do we get over it?

I can't speak for them. What about you?

Well today I ate in public, and went to the library. And lately I've been out more with friends. In the morning I'm not real sure what to do unless I have a specific appointment. I still have no "normal" schedule. But talking to you helps.

I'm glad.

No really, you help me sort out my thoughts and listen to how I feel. I'm not as apprehensive as I was. I think I'm getting braver.

Stacks

There was a stack of papers taking up space on my kitchen counter. Assorted stuff that piled up since the last time I cleaned off the limited work area a few months ago. There are stacks like this all over my house and they could easily overwhelm me, if I let them.

So while waiting on the microwave to heat a cup of coffee, my mind swirling around unclear thoughts, I tried tackling the nearby stack.

I couldn't find a new place for everything in that counter stack. I threw some things away, moved others to another stack, and put one on the refrigerator (which is just another form of stack). When I was finished there was still a stack on the kitchen counter, but it was smaller.

Feeling somewhat accomplished after sorting through the disorganized pile, I walked into one of the spare bedrooms. It has no bed or any clear purpose, except to hold stacks. It also contained the boxes of Carlton's things, as it used to be his bedroom. My eyes scanned the room and rested on a table full of stacks. On top was the envelope I received from California nearly four months after Kelly's phone call. It contained official copies of the death certificate and the coroner's report, stating "multi-drug intoxication" as the cause of death. A wave of nausea rose in my stomach and I slowly backed out of the room. This was not a project for that day.

I tried the next bedroom, which actually has a bed but would be of little use to a guest because it is also covered in stacks. There were books, watercolors, sketch pads, and journals — products from my creative endeavors. I understood the purpose of this room better, so I lingered long enough to begin clearing the bed for potential company by skimming papers and remembering when I wrote them or why. I took several of them into the sunroom to set next to the computer.

I was not exactly sure what my plan was for these writings; they just needed to be near the computer.

In the sunroom I became sidetracked leafing through another stack on top of the half-empty file cabinet, until the dryer buzzed from the laundry closet. I set the papers down and walked toward the sound. I pulled out warm towels and folded them, then took them to the linen closet in the front bathroom near the guestroom. The bed in that room was still not completely clear, and there was a new stack by the computer in the sunroom, but my towels were clean and put away.

This mess didn't happen overnight. To think I could dig through it in one determined effort was to invite frustration. Little by little I have excavated the stacks, letting them take me where I needed to go.

It's a metaphor for my life now, chipping away at old memories, accumulated in no discernible order. I am constantly choosing what to let go of, what to find a new place for, and what to leave for another day.

On my computer there is a program called de-fragmenting. I turn on the "details" while it scans one line at a time, cleaning up pieces of scattered information. Sometimes it seems to hit a snag and send the search all the way back to the beginning. This is similar to my grief journey. I would make it through a couple of "good" hours or days, sorting through my life, increasing my pace, thinking I was back on solid ground.

Then wham! a sad memory or a wave of anxiety would knock me back to what felt like the beginning.

This book evolved the same way. I would work on one little story, only to be reminded of two others. Sorting through the accumulation of memories seemed to have no order. Often I have felt I was running in circles, but I wasn't yet ready to give up. I visualized a spiral, spinning outward in an ever-widening arc to replace this mindless, tail-chasing image.

Life hasn't been a simple walk down a clear, straight path. When I let go of that idea, the journey becomes more of an adventure and the scenery more enjoyable. These triggered recollections of 55 years are showing me all the whimsical diversions and rich layers of the experience known as Laura Flett.

Cleaning House

My house is comfortable, but it's a mess. In addition to the books and papers resting on every available horizontal plane, clothes drape over chairs and a light dust covers every surface.

When Carlton was young, Saturday mornings were designated for cleaning the house. I became Dragon Lady, lighting fires under husband and son, expecting everyone else's schedule to fall in line with mine. No one was happy. The house might get straightened, but we were all a mess.

Now I live alone, except for the shedding Princess. I no longer have the rigid schedule telling me Saturday morning is the only time this house can be cleaned. There is no one to blame for the clutter but myself. Well, I have pointed out that the dog's toys are scattered throughout the house, but no more than any of my things.

Somehow I've moved past the mindset that my house needs to look a certain way, no longer caring as much about how presentable it is. I guess that happened soon after I realized it was now all my responsibility.

On an afternoon when a friend was to stop by, I ran the vacuum cleaner in the living room, took the kitchen garbage outside to the compost bin, dusted with a lemon scented spray and loaded the dishwasher with the last 24 hours of dirty dishes. It only took about twenty minutes, and the front rooms really did look and smell better.

When the cable man came to fix my Internet connection, the sunroom, where my computer resides, got its own twenty-minute cleaning. I ran a dustmop over the tile floor littered with birdseed and feathers from the dove's cage, emptied an overflowing trash can of paper, and closed the louvered doors to the laundry closet full of detergent bottles, empty hangers, and dirty clothes. It didn't take much, but it was a noticeable improvement.

Sometimes I do hit a limit on how much mess I can live with. This usually happens when I can't find last month's electric bill, or I've tripped over scattered books and toys one too many times. So I whip into a cleaning frenzy for an hour or two, until I feel more organized, or have at least found the nearly-overdue bill.

A bright yellow sign was hung on my kitchen doorknob advertising window washing and gutter cleaning. Yeah, that was a pleasant image. I've had my windows professionally washed before and the whole house sparkled. But I never called them, even though their sign hung on the door for a month.

In a television interview J. K. Rowling admitted to living in absolute squalor for five years while she wrote her first Harry Potter novel. I can picture a rather creative mess piling up around her as she spun her magical story. I liked that scene and have often borrowed the quote to explain myself.

If the mess isn't making me anxious, then it must be at an acceptable level for me, and balance is what I am looking for. I'm learning how to identify what I can live with, rather than just reacting to an outside standard that sets off inside fireworks.

An interesting thing happened the day an out-of-town friend dropped by unexpectedly. I hadn't seen her in a while and I immediately launched into my knee-jerk apology for the mess, closing a bedroom door and sliding a stack of books to the floor so she had a place to sit down. My friend countered with a lengthy description of her own messy house, as if we were finalists for the coveted Slob of the Year title. Cute. Later, replaying the competitive conversation in my head, I had the thought: Maybe we could start a new trend.

All the wasted energy on those Saturday mornings long ago, when no one really wanted to be cleaning, can't be called back. I was trying to please some perceived outside authority. For now I can just be careful not to waste any more time worrying about it. I want this house to feel safe as I'm busy cleaning up my inner mess. The outer mess will get the attention it needs, as it needs it.

Two-Part Harmony

Carolyn, a childhood friend, called to offer a trip away from the safety of my home. She wanted me to go with her to the Maine coast for a week in October 2003, to see the fall foliage. I had never done this, and she had made the trip several times. She would find a house to rent and her daughter, who worked for Delta, could get plane tickets for next to nothing. I knew Carolyn liked this kind of detail decision-making more than I, but I soon discovered that even deciding whether or not to go was too hard for me. I took my uncertainty to the notebook.

Carolyn used to be very outgoing. She might overwhelm me.

That was years ago. How is she now?

Well, she's been living alone for a while. And she knows my introverted side. We had a good time in that mountain cabin in North Carolina a few years ago.

Then this could be fun too. Talk to her about it.

So I did. We talked about what we might do up there for a week. I wanted to be assured that the adventure wouldn't be too structured, and I found we both just needed a healthy dose of Mother Nature and a break from our own responsibilities. I decided this could work.

It was an invigorating experience, staying for a week in a quaint cottage by the Atlantic Ocean in the tiny town of Friendship, Maine. I chose an upstairs bedroom, a loft with a slanting ceiling and a view of the water, furnished with stenciled furniture and a quilt-topped bed. I took Madeline L'Engle's *Two-Part Invention* up there to read. I tested my old scouting skills at the fireplace downstairs in the living room, gathering tinder and kindling from the nearby woods.

We drove to neighboring towns, pulling off the road to take pictures of the colorful scenery and wandering in and out of bookstores and craft shops in little villages along the way. We spent a brisk afternoon at the lighthouse, Carolyn's favorite spot, watching the ocean crash into the rocks. On another afternoon we ate fresh clam chowder at a local café. Carolyn and I cooked and shared most evening meals, refrigerating leftover chicken stew and salads for individual grazing later. We spent hours quietly sitting in the same room with our books and journals. Or we ventured out alone for solitary walks through the neighborhood of multi-colored trees, collecting leaves to preserve as memories.

It was perfect. I couldn't have guessed Carolyn would offer me my first extended opportunity to tiptoe back into the world. Life keeps putting people on my journey I am willing to trust, with lessons I am ready to learn. Carolyn, once choir director at our church, sang the soprano of our duet while I, the alto, practiced finding sustained harmony in the presence of another.

But even though we had a shared history and were successfully spending time together, we talked around the death of Carlton, using "God words" for generalities, and avoiding the specifics of our personal pain. Was this also part of our history, the feelings we were told as children not to share? I was saving most of my emotional ramblings for the safety of my notebook, still unsure how to connect with another person. It wasn't until the second-to-last day in Maine that I felt comfortable enough to venture deeper into the conversation. I was grateful she hadn't pushed. She has two children about Carlton's age, who were his friends, and she had a big brother Tommy who died of cancer in his early thirties. I asked her when Tommy had died.

January 11. The same day Carlton died. She probably knew that all along and was just waiting for me to ask.

Birthday on the Beach

In the middle of November 2003, my family was closing in on me. Dad was put in the hospital because his heartbeat was irregular and the doctor wanted to explore the possibility of a pacemaker. I agreed to meet my brother Bruce at the registration desk to help check Dad in, then ended up spending the night in his hospital room to prevent him from trying to leave, like he had done on a previous occasion. I did this for the family, the responsibility I still felt as the "big sister." However, in the morning I was tired and grumpy from sleeping on a plastic loveseat, listening for sounds of escape. All I wanted to do was go home, take a bath, and crawl into my own bed. Unfortunately the doctor made his morning rounds before I could leave and very emphatically told me that someone needed to stay with Dad. After the doctor left the room, I waited about ten minutes, went home, and called Bruce. I repeated the doctor's instructions and confessed I couldn't stay another night. Later that afternoon when I delivered clean clothes to the nurses' station they told me Dad was doing fine, so I slipped away.

November 28, 2003, would have been Carlton's twenty-eighth birthday. I wanted some time to myself, but it was beginning to look like the only way this could happen was to get out of town. I remembered the trip with Carolyn a month earlier as a refreshing change of scenery, and my chaotic family doing fine without me. I went to the Internet to explore a getaway route and ended up booking a room at the pet-friendly Holiday Inn Express on the Biloxi beach. I envisioned myself on the Mississippi coast in the warm sunshine with Princess for company and my books and notebooks for some serious work on my collection of school stories.

I began the seven-hour road trip, heading east on Interstate 20. The farther I got from Shreveport, the better I felt. Maybe this was the feeling Carlton had when he started his drive to the West Coast — a way to untangle from the web of Fletts. I decided within the first hour that I would stay as long as I needed to. Bruce had the motel's phone number; they would be fine without me.

After driving across northern Louisiana and through the bottom half of Mississippi, my hotel room, with its little refrigerator, microwave, HBO and coffeemaker, was just perfect. I never realized how welcome maroon paisley bedspreads and mass-produced artwork bolted to the wall could be. I set up my computer on the desk, spread out an assortment of books on one bed, stretched out on the other, and promptly fell asleep. Two hours later, after the refreshing nap, I walked a couple blocks down Highway 90 to a seafood restaurant for dinner then returned "home" with a Styrofoam doggy bag containing enough fried fish and French fries for a second meal. After putting it in the little refrigerator, I crawled back into bed. I could work on the book in the morning, when I was more rested.

The next day was cool and overcast, and the HBO guide on top of the television advertised two movies of interest. I showered, dressed, and wandered to the motel lobby for a fairly substantial "free" breakfast. After helping myself to Danishes, orange juice, coffee, boiled eggs, and a banana for later, I returned to the room and leashed my loyal companion for a brisk morning walk down the highway. When we returned to the room, I released the princess, kicked off my shoes, crawled under the warm covers, and grabbed the remote. I would work later.

But after two movies and a leftover fish lunch, the motel walls began to close in on me. I got in the car for a drive down the highway to Ocean Springs, a bedroom community across the Biloxi Bay, and the setting of my first teaching job in 1971. I was a young hippie then and remembered the little town being rather cool and arty. It was still a bedroom community, but now it was full of little boutiques and restaurants, appearing a bit more yuppie-like. Maybe this was the current definition of cool and arty.

When I returned to the motel room, I flipped through some of the books spread out on the second bed. Nothing held my attention for more than five minutes, so I picked up my journal.

I'm not working. But I'll be staying a couple more days. There's still plenty of time.

On the third morning the sun broke through, luring me out into its warmth. I hurriedly dressed, returned to the lobby for the "free" breakfast and another banana, then grabbed my bag of notebooks and pens. My plan was to spend most of the day walking up and down the beach. This was, after all, what I had imagined when first planning the getaway. The effort of picking up one foot and then the other on the sandy beach reminded me of other beaches I have walked. In a casual restaurant overlooking the water, with an oyster poboy and a cold bottle of beer, I noted mammoth casinos on piers looming in the distance, where grand hotels and fancy restaurants once perched. On the walk back, there was another sense of *déjà vu* while wandering in and out of half a dozen souvenir shops packed with t-shirts and shells. When I returned to the room, I didn't even think about book work; my mind and journal were busy recalling a full day of observations and pleasant feelings.

By the fourth day I was beginning to get restless.

I've been unwinding in the sun's energy and my
memories long enough. Obviously I did not come
to work. Maybe I was looking for something else,
like an excuse to play, and beaches held fond
memories of where I have played.

Packing my car to begin the trip home, I noticed how relaxed I felt. There was no anxiety churning in my stomach, no thoughts spinning in my head. The witness of my journal told me I had been doing exactly what I needed to do, accomplishing little in conventionally productive ways, but a great deal in the way of taking care of myself. Heading home, I saw myself as spider, the Indian symbol for storyteller, ready to return to the web without getting tangled in it.

Role Models

My poor Daddy. He bumped his head on a low branch of the large, spreading magnolia tree in front of the family home a couple of weeks before the Flett family reunion was to convene here in 2001. From Milbank, South Dakota, he was the last of seven children and a son of the town's doctor during the Great Depression. His nieces and nephews and their grown children were coming to Shreveport, many for the very first time.

Daddy ended up in Shreveport, after spending four years in the South Pacific during World War II, supposedly because he couldn't face another Midwestern winter. My parents were both in radio broadcasting in the late '40s. They met and fell in love across a crowded room. Or so the story went. Mom, a first-generation Southern belle (her parents originally being from Pennsylvania), created this lifetime role while majoring in drama at LSU.

Our little '50s family grew up with the models of Ozzie and Harriet Nelson and June and Ward Cleaver as the ideal American families. Did we ever question whether or not Ozzie had a job? Or how June Cleaver could clean house in her heels and pearls? And when Wally was in trouble his parents never looked as upset as ours. My family must have been ahead of its time, appearing much more like those portrayed later in *All in the Family*, with its grumpy father and eager-to-please wife. Or *Wonder Years*, whose parents seemed constantly overwhelmed by the adolescent angst of their children.

But in 2001, when Dad bumped his head — on a Southern magnolia tree, no less — it triggered something that had been lurking just below the surface all these years. And it was happening at the time the Flett family was finally coming south to visit.

For the next year-and-a-half, Dad declined, as he angrily fought the confusion swirling around him. It was a new experience for the whole family, and we tried, each in our own way, to respond the best we knew how. Rage in him, a practicing alcoholic, was not new. But this time was different. My brothers and I, each facing middle-age challenges, had adult responsibilities of our own. We were not sure how involved we could afford to be.

Dad's decline was taking its toll on Mom, too, the Southern belle caregiver, whose skills included hosting ladies' luncheons and singing in the church choir. Her coquettish ways weren't working. She believed he was "acting" this way on purpose, or just being stubborn. Of course, the mental breakdown she experienced my senior year in high school seemed to reinforce her own stubbornness, which she willingly held on to. She argued that he had not been officially diagnosed with Alzheimer's by the family doctor and refused any further information. We were at a stalemate.

Our family was still fragile from the death of Carlton, but by the end of 2003 we knew it was time to make some drastic changes. We looked to each other to see who was willing to take the lead. My brothers and I had initiated a family discussion several months earlier, dropping hints of how living arrangements might need to change for the health and safety of everyone involved. I was not eager to take on much else, not sure of my own stamina. My business-like brother Bruce and my good-old-boy brother Buddy found a place for Dad at the War Veterans Nursing Home in Monroe. With the help of the family doctor, who prescribed Antabuse to control Dad's drinking, a plan was set. This was a decision the children had to make without Mother.

Buddy and I arrived at their house to take Dad to the VA for a checkup. We just neglected to tell them it was the VA one hundred miles away. Once we were on the Interstate I called Bruce, and he and his wife went to Mother's to pack a bag, and deliver the news that "they" wanted to keep him for a few days, then got on the highway to meet up with us in Monroe.

My poor dad watched the scenery pass from the front passenger seat on the drive to Monroe. His younger son Buddy (Deane, Jr.) assured him that we were almost there, just as Dad used to tell us on family vacations. I sat quietly in the back, unsure of my role, my pen noting pieces of conversation and observations. I also checked the electronic Amber Alert highway sign we passed, informing motorists of missing children, to see if Dad's name was on it.

After an hour-and-a-half we arrived at the attractive modern facility with a fishing pier and pecan orchards. Registration paperwork and a doctor's check-up took a couple of hours. Then it was time for us to leave. Dad looked so helpless and confused when we told him good-bye. This was hard, even with a kind staff assuring us he would be in good hands, and my brothers and I remembering what life had been like for quite some time at the family home. With tear-stained faces we told ourselves that this was for the best, commented on how clean and friendly the nursing home seemed, and avoided each other's eyes. While we were busy justifying it to ourselves, we wondered aloud how we would explain it to Mother.

When we got back to Shreveport we gave her a brief synopsis of the event. Just the facts, as we knew them. He was there on a trial basis, to see if this was a workable solution. Her vivid imagination filled in the gaps. After a few weeks on her own, she began to appreciate the calmer environment, and no further explanation was needed.

It has taken time and practice to adjust to this new phase in our family's life. One or more of us makes a day trip to Monroe every two weeks, then passes the news to the rest of the family. And we watch other veterans, besides Dad, in different stages of their own war stories.

Dad silently sits in the dayroom with no particular assignment, and Mom has her empty castle back under her control. There are no longer circular discussions about the difference between Alzheimer's and dementia, or 911 calls in the middle of the night when he falls out of bed, or anxious imaginings about what else could possibly happen. Our little family has accepted the fact that we could never make that *Donna Reed* image fit.

Having witnessed my parents' identity crisis, I approached mid-life with a fear that I was also hiding behind a role that no longer fit. I was eager not to follow my parents' footsteps and my journal was the friend who appeared to show me a way to get to know myself better.

Cruising

About a year after Carlton's death I was invited to be a chaperone for some high school Girl Scouts going on a Caribbean cruise. I fondly remembered my own Girl Scout trip to Mexico, overland to the Cabana, a Scout hostel. Two of these young ladies had been enthusiastic second graders in my science class, and when they were in middle school I went camping with their troop. When one of the leader/mothers couldn't go, Patricia, the other leader, remembered me and called.

She and I would take five sophomore and junior girls to Cozumel and Costa Maya, Mexico, aboard a Royal Caribbean cruise ship during spring break. I didn't know much about cruises, but I did know high school girls probably wouldn't want to be roped into working on merit badges. I picked up my notebook.

Can I handle being stuck on a boat in the middle of the Gulf of Mexico with a couple thousand people for five days after a year of near solitude? Won't I be overwhelmed?

Not if you don't want to be. What can you do ahead of time?

I can talk to my friend Erma. She's been on a couple of cruises and she's an introvert.

That's a good idea. What else?

I can take you along for company.

Great. I'd love to go. I've never been on a cruise before either.

Three of the teenagers were assigned to a tiny cabin with me. The miniature bathroom and closets crowded the entrance. Two bunk beds at the other end of the room were separated by a narrow passage that led into a small sitting area in the middle large enough for a loveseat on one side, a dresser/dressing table on the other and a cumbersome coffee table with sharp corners filling the center. Patricia, another adult, and the two other scouts were in a second cabin down the hall. I handed out room cards to "my girls," claimed a bottom bunk and a part of the closet, then proceeded to look over the schedule of events for the evening. The young women, all very responsible, followed suit and the adventure began.

Each morning I climbed over erupting cargo bags and suitcases that covered the limited floor space to wake up teenagers with a simple "good morning," then stood back and allowed them to emerge in their own unique ways. For five days they roamed the ship, went to activities designed for teens, lay out on the deck, ate, shopped for souvenirs at the ports, and had their own special vacation. Patricia and I sunbathed, people-watched, ate, explored the adult on-board activities, and went shopping. I continued to amaze myself with active participation.

We met as a troop at our assigned table for formal evening dinners, tried escargot and calamari for the first time and shamelessly ordered two different desserts apiece. Afterwards we watched elaborate stage shows in the auditorium, the adolescents sitting on the opposite side of the large room. In Cozumel we snorkeled the clear blue Gulf waters together, looking for Nemo. We gathered for lunch and shopping in Casa Maya, and assembled on the circular staircase in the middle of the ship on the return trip home for an appointment with a professional photographer. But most of the time Patricia and I just passed the teenagers on our way to a line dance class, as they participated in a stem-to-stern scavenger hunt.

Periodically I pulled away for quiet time in the small, deserted ship library to write in my notebook, or slipped into the minuscule cabin for a quick nap, then later met up with others in our group for ongoing grazing at the continuous buffet or to listen to a variety of musicians in one of several lounges.

All of us were taking charge of our own good time, finding what we needed and wanted from this trip. I quickly learned to do the give-and-take dance with a roomful of high school girls and a boatload of strangers.

No one on this ship knew about Carlton's death. Even Patricia, who knew I had a son. On the last full day of the trip as we enjoyed a leisurely lunch, she casually asked about him.

I stammered for words and my eyes filled with tears. I told her briefly what had happened. There were several moments of awkward silence, as we both searched for something else to talk about.

I later noted the incident in my composition book, as I reviewed the fun I had had around all these people. The trip was exactly what was needed. A break from Laura the grieving mother. And a chance to be Laura, cruising.

Carlton's
Kindergarten
Picture

Photo by Cowen Studios of Shreveport LA

Carlton Harris
Captain Shreve High School
Class of 1994

Connections

Stoner Hill

I took my scruffy dog, the albino dove, and one lone tetra fish to Leah's kindergarten class to teach a lesson comparing and contrasting "fur, feathers, and fins." The dove and fish were former occupants of Nature Lab, the hands-on science class I taught for the younger children at Stoner Hill Elementary School until retiring in May 2001.

I was first hired at this school as a science teacher for the fourth and fifth grades while their regular teacher was on sabbatical. Because she was returning for the next year, the position was not permanent. However, when an enrichment teacher's job for the younger grades became available, I volunteered to develop an extension of the science program. The principal agreed to the idea and left me on my own to clean out a cluttered classroom used for storage, develop an activity-based curriculum, and find materials to teach science concepts through inquiry. For six years that was my all-consuming passion.

Outside the classroom we grew fall and spring vegetable gardens. At one end of the campus we planted sixty saplings for an arboretum. Inside the classroom, in the company of a diversity of caged animals, we experimented with sound and light, hot and cold, liquids and solids, and discovered "doing" science was much more fun than just listening and watching. We traced the changes in water by dancing the "Water Cycle Boogie" and learned to measure carefully by making gingerbread in a Dixie cup. I was learning at least as much as any student assigned to this class.

Walking to Leah's room with the caged bird on a sunny day in 2004, I passed a line of second graders eager to greet my feathered friend. Some of them knew the mama bird when they were four-year-olds in my classroom. They remembered her as the one who laid eggs and laughed. It was a connection more than half a lifetime ago for these cherub children.

After leaving the bird in the kindergarten classroom, I went back to my car for Princess and the fish bowl and decided to return to the room using a different route, hoping to keep disturbances to a minimum. The nature lady walking a frisky dog down the breezeway might possibly stir up whirlwinds of excited children. We passed twelve-foot trees planted once upon a time by my little foresters. Continuing, we traveled over a hill of barren schoolyard where the organic vegetable garden had been. Walking around the end of the building took us past my old classroom.

There stood a 25-pound birdseed bucket full of blooming orange amaryllis — another remnant of Nature Lab.

Stoner Hill Elementary School sits on one of the highest "hills" in our otherwise flat northwest Louisiana city. To the east is the Red River, dividing us from the neighboring town of Bossier City. To the north is the downtown business area. To the south and west are large residential areas.

Captain Henry Miller Shreve settled the town of Shreveport in the 1830s after breaking up a logjam in the river at the bottom of this hill not far from where my own logjam began breaking up. Stoner Hill was the sacred ground where I became aware of the seeds I could plant in small children, and where I allowed children to plant seeds in me.

Writing for the Market

I retired from teaching to write a book about my experiences in Nature Lab, entitled *Paying Attention in Class: One Teacher's Story*. It was a collection of lessons from children, animals and the great outdoors that I had learned and wanted to share. But I couldn't find a publisher. The education presses sent me form letters explaining how it didn't fit their needs. I wasn't sure what that meant.

It was discouraging. The current emphasis in education seemed to be about improving test scores. Hands-on ideas were popular five years earlier. I wanted to scream to anyone willing to listen that education is a process, and no one idea is separate, to be discarded for another. What was this intense focus on scores, overriding educators' knowledge of child development, learning styles, and the once-popular philosophy of teaching the whole child? Maybe I should have made that clearer.

Maybe I should have described the student population where I taught. It was a low socio-economic minority school, halfway between a popular private school and an academic magnet public high school. Many of my young students lived undetected in the high-crime area of a government housing project across the street from the high school. Their families, often headed by a single parent or grandparent, were victims and perpetrators of abuse and neglect. These children didn't have pets, or go to camp, or dig in their backyards. They couldn't even play safely outside.

It was my belief that all children could benefit from an interactive class such as mine, and it was my intention to recognize the universal gift of creative play in children. Perhaps the importance of a class like this would have been easier to recognize if the reader knew who my students were.

But when presenting district or state workshops I regularly met with teachers who told me that too much activity doesn't work at their school; their children were too "low." Again, I felt the urge to scream. Sure it won't work, if that's what you believe. Was I willing to say that in those workshops?

Many of my most enthusiastic students struggled in their reading and math classes, but mine, a magical room inviting imagination and creative effort, seemed to be a natural fit for the curiosity and wonder all children innately have.

Would Carlton have had different survival skills if I had encouraged his creative side? I regularly affirmed his test-taking skills and logical thinking, the emphasis I was now questioning. Nature Lab began the year of his first suicide attempt. Was I offering an environment for children that my own son yearned for? Was this why I began to pay closer attention to the needs of the children around me? Was he asking to be included in this quest for the universal child? Wasn't this a class that I, the avid Girl Scout camper, would have enjoyed? The questions are overwhelming.

Should I rewrite my first book, describing my particular students in an effort to make it more marketable? Can't I find another way to convince the education presses that all children need opportunities to celebrate their creativity? Will I ever be able to explain this passion so people can hear me?

I do know that the two-and-a-half years I spent writing about my classroom experiences was a constant reminder of my own creative urge and the preparation I needed to help my scared inner child learn her lessons when she was faced with the death of her only birth child.

Looking for Playmates

I felt such emptiness when I looked at pictures of Carlton as a young child. He was so full of life. One photo, taken when he was three, shows his light blond bowl-shaped haircut framing big blue eyes and wide grin. His arms spread open. The little boy who asked endless questions and ran everywhere he went. He was the precious child I was given to share life and joy with. My tears told me to pick up my pen.

My heart hurts. What do I do now that this magical playmate is gone?

It's time for a reality check, Laura. He hasn't been that little boy for a long time. He was looking for his own joy and reason to appreciate life.

I guess we all are.

With my illusion destroyed, I have had to be more creative when looking for playmates. I welcome the chance to interact with young children. Part of my job as teacher was to rein in some of their unbridled joy in order to teach school skills. It was hard to fully appreciate what they had to offer when I was so busy imposing my adult world on them. This was probably why volunteering in Leah's kindergarten class once a week was much more fun. I could drop in for a couple of hours, play as hard as possible, make magic and silliness and a general mess, then leave, Tinkerbell-like, as Leah lined them up for an orderly walk to lunch. I worried the longer these cherubs stayed in school walking in straight lines and preparing for standardized tests, the less likely they could remain playmates, for me or for each other.

My frisky Princess is a good playmate. She runs full throttle in circles around the house with a pink flamingo Beanie Baby dangling from her mouth, then collapses into a fluffy puddle, snuggling beside me while I write. Our leisurely walks are more my preference, as she stops to smell the roses and everything else along the path.

Adult playmates can be harder to find. We are busy with images to protect, schedules to meet, and bills to pay. Maybe we learned those adult things when we were in school. I exercise caution when approaching these "grown-ups," hoping to find someone with whom to play. We give ourselves permission to be more relaxed unwinding at happy hour on Friday, or listening to music, or celebrating birthdays. But other occasions are trickier, as we gather to discuss study skills or writing, or salvation, or hold forums to solve the community's education problems. Such settings can be challenging to our playfulness when we are taking ourselves so seriously.

If I begin to wilt in a room full of heavy, hot air, I look for a way to lighten the atmosphere, so I can breathe again. I listen for cues, watch for breaks, or wait for an invitation. Sometimes it never comes and I decide the environment is too stifling for me. Sometimes I find playing in my head is enough; I just have to remember not to laugh out loud at inappropriate moments. And sometimes, with a bit of luck and attention, I find the opening I've been waiting for — another playmate waiting for a cue, a chance to release a chuckle or two, or an opportunity to comment on the silliness over the plight of things in general.

I continue to look for playmates because I truly believe that hiding deep inside all these adult-form straight guys, myself included, are playful children just waiting to be invited outside.

So what do I do when I can't find anyone to play with? Well, as little Laura waits patiently for an outside invitation, Mama Laura looks within and finds a most compatible partner, the little girl she knows best. She is careful not to take herself too seriously or overwhelm her child with suffocating rules, as we two learn to play together as one.

A Change of Plans

It was raining outside, and I couldn't walk in the park. The inconvenience convinced me I could get through another day without going to the grocery store, but I grumbled to myself, wondering how to release the cabin fever that was building inside me.

When I was an elementary teacher, rainy days meant "inside recess," which also meant lots of noise from board games or a class game of 7-Up. There was no recess from teacher mode either. I was expected to monitor the games for cheaters and peekers, and the only way for me to go to the bathroom was to pair up with the teacher next door and one of us watch two classes at a time.

As a science enrichment teacher I found rainy days a different kind of challenge. Many of our activities took place outside. If it was raining, board games or 7-Up didn't cover the lesson's objectives. I needed an effective way to teach inside the classroom and still make it motivating and fun. I needed a Plan B.

It was a practice in flexibility and learning to accept what is. Successful teachers know they must adjust and work with what they have, but having a Plan B is for more than just the classroom. It's for times when life in general isn't going quite the way we expected.

When I retired, I visualized telling the story of my teaching experience in a novel way and seeing it in print. I envisioned myself featured on *Oprah* as the clever teacher who put the fun back into learning. I saw myself confidently sitting on her sofa chatting away with the equally self-assured hostess, as we solved the problems of the nation's public school system. She has yet to call, but then no education publishers have scooped up my ideas either. One editor's rejection letter was kind enough to suggest I submit my manuscript to memoir presses, but I haven't found a connection there, either.

I didn't plan for my second attempt at writing a book to follow the death of my only child. I thought he had found his path and would be climbing the computer career ladder in sunny southern California for quite some time. But this did not happen. I needed a Plan B.

What will I do today? It's rainy.

Is that a bad thing?

I can't go walking in the park. Just getting out seems too much trouble.

Maybe it's a Plan B day, a chance to discover another way to entertain yourself. Put your clever little teaching philosophy to work and find the fun in learning.

Storyteller

In the summer of 2001, after retiring from 30 years of teaching, I went to a writing workshop in Taos, New Mexico. The teacher, Natalie Goldberg, was the author of two of my favorite writing books, *Writing Down the Bones* and *Wild Mind*. Natalie's book jacket biography tells of workshops she gives and includes a website address. Eager to learn everything

I could about being a writer, I went to the computer, made my reservation for the next one offered and sent in a deposit. In early July I drove my trusty four-cylinder, air-conditioned Toyota Corolla across the endless hot, dry plains of Texas, eager to begin my new path. I planned to spend a day exploring the shops and galleries of Santa Fe before going to the workshop in Taos.

I wanted a storyteller, the southwestern culture's clay figure with a lapful of children. The role of storyteller seemed like the logical transition for me, as I moved from teacher to writer. And although I searched many stores, none of the figurines seemed to connect. I really wanted to like one or another, but something was not quite right about each one. Those

Little Laura

with misbehaving children didn't appeal to my schoolteacher self, and the chubby matrons didn't look enough like me.

I left Santa Fe the next day for an early arrival in Taos to continue the search for a storyteller figure and again had no luck. It was time to let go of that idea and settle in at the Mabel Dodge Luhan House for a week of intense writing practice. This lodge, a gathering place for Georgia O'Keefe, Willa Cather, D.H. Lawrence, Ansel Adams and others, was where I watched with awe as my magical pen, under Natalie's guidance, joined the universal dance. Ah. The workshop was what I had come for.

The following Christmas, in my new life as a writer, I gave each of my teacher friends a candle wrapped in an angel-adorned ribbon and the advice not to burn it at both ends. It was what I was learning for myself in retirement. When Kathy sent me a thank-you card with a storyteller on the front, I put it on my refrigerator. The picture next to her note was of me as a small child sitting in a rocking chair reading to my dolls. Me! A storyteller! Maybe I've been one all my life.

Three-and-a-half years later, in May 2004, I traveled to Boulder, Colorado, to begin a year-long commitment with a long-distance writing group, focused on completing a book. I already had a manuscript of school stories, but felt I needed outside help writing a book about my son's death. I also hoped to avoid the discouraging pile of rejection form letters from my first book that were collecting in my guest room. The biggest attractions for signing up, however, were the writing teachers, Sean Murphy and his wife Tania Casselle. Sean had been a co-teacher with Natalie in that summer of 2001, and I had fond memories of his quiet encouragement.

I drove to Boulder, retracing my path through New Mexico, and again allowing time in Santa Fe and Taos. I still wanted a storyteller doll and began wandering in and out of stores with that same unsettled feeling. I walked into a Santa Fe gift shop, and a clerk named Mary stepped forward and asked if she could help. I told her I was looking for a storyteller doll with no misbehaving children. She showed me a lovely standing figure dressed in blue with a long dark braid down her back. Her eyes are cast heavenward, and the six happy children holding on to her were all behaving. I liked her immediately.

"The doll was made by a nineteen-year-old young man named Clayton whose mother also makes storytellers," Mary explained.

Something stirred inside me when I heard it was made by the son. Even the name sounded familiar. I was not yet sure what I had found and decided to continue my search. But nothing compared to what Mary had shown me.

Tired and hungry, I stopped for lunch. While picking at my organic salad of field greens, sun-dried tomatoes, feta cheese, and walnuts, I could think only of Clayton's storyteller. The proud upright woman. The contented children. It was the doll I had been looking for. I finished eating, paid, then quickly returned to the shop. Maybe I had not been ready for her until I realized how much I needed her help to tell the story about my own son Carlton.

The storyteller now stands silently beside me on the table by my blue-flowered sofa, looking up at the skylights, with happy children holding on to her, lending me courage to keep pushing my pen.

Metaphors

I, the neophyte writer, and he, living in Hollywood, the movie capital of the world, were struggling to find a way to communicate, so one way Carlton and I connected during our infrequent phone conversations was by discussing books and movies. We talked about the books we were reading. Two of his favorite authors, Kurt Vonnegut and Fyodor Dostoevsky, had been mine when I was his age. And when he began quoting the Gnostic book, the *Gospel of Thomas*, I checked out a copy from the library.

But most of the conversations were about movies. Carlton went to new releases every Saturday morning and belonged to a movie rental service, so he was a very good source for recommendations. When he suggested a movie I might like, I would rent it as soon as possible so we could talk about it in a future conversation.

We considered *Mulholland Drive* a story about reincarnation, or at least reliving your life with a chance to make different choices. After watching *The Matrix* we both expressed a desire to escape our own perceived entanglements.

I rented *Minority Report* on his recommendation and told him in a later phone call that I identified with the older woman in the greenhouse. She developed the program that nursed the pre-ops back to health and released them into the world. It reminded me of my job as a public school teacher, helping nurture the minds of the students, and then releasing them into the real world. Maybe he was seeing himself as a pre-op. He didn't say. I didn't ask.

The Red Violin and *13 Conversations about One Thing* were several stories woven together as a spider, the storyteller, might spin into a web, a technique I was beginning to relate to.

K-PAX, *The Sixth Sense*, and *Signs* were movies alluding to a greater force, something beyond what we see. What were you trying to tell me, Son? Or were you asking? Is it something you believed? Or wanted to believe? I liked the movies and the idea of this greater plan, but I wasn't able to give Carlton any absolute assurance about it. I was still looking for it myself.

The last e-mail I got from Carlton was a list of movie recommendations. *Best in Show, Quiz Show, Bowling for Columbine, Waking Life*. It was several months before I had the courage to rent them. I intensely watched each one, searching for clues, a defining theme, anything relevant. Looking for an assurance of a greater plan. Was this a collection of man's search for meaning? Could I not hear what you were saying, Carlton? Was part of your frustration not being able to communicate with me? What were we missing in our own conversations by letting someone else's movies and books tell our stories?

All I really know now is my interpretation of what Carlton was trying to tell me and my own inner child spirit's story.

During our final phone conversation, Carlton asked me if I knew why I was here. Because I was immersed in my story of Nature Lab at that time, I told him I thought I was here to connect children with nature.

"Yeah, Mom," he said, "listen to the children."

"I'm trying," I replied, unsure what he meant by that. I wish I had asked.

He asked if he was in the book. I proudly assured him he was all the way through it and actually named several times.

He told me he didn't know why he was here in the world. He said he didn't feel very creative.

"I felt that way at your age. It's a temporary feeling," I answered, perhaps too quickly.

I didn't remember how hopeless that "temporary" feeling was in my mid-twenties. I could have told him how hard teaching was and how scared I was that I had chosen the wrong career. I could have mentioned how tired I was of being a bridesmaid in all my friends' weddings, without a prospective partner of my own. Or told him that I was so sad at the age of 23 I swallowed a dozen aspirin, then panicked and called the poison control hotline. Unfortunately during this conversation, I was fighting my own uncertain feelings of career choices, love options, and concerns about whether or not I wanted to hold on. I, the menopausal woman, was doubting her own ability to create.

I didn't know how to listen to my son. I didn't know how to talk to him. I was busy listening to myself, learning how to talk to me. I wish now I had said, "You were here, Dear One, as my outer child to teach me of the child spirit each of us carries within. You gave my life purpose when I needed it most. You validated my ability to create."

We talked to each other through the metaphors of books and movies. Then he left for his next adventure, and my job became storyteller, to weave together as honestly and clearly as I could, the story of Carlton and Laura and all the other children looking for their own creative natures.

Tears

I had no tears and little feeling for days after the phone call from Kelly. In fact I was terrified that if I ever started crying I would never be able to stop. For months I lived obsessed with this fear. I allowed myself a few tears in private, or in the bathroom of a friend's house or public building, but that was all I was willing to risk. What caused this fear?

I've probably stuffed tears all my life. My mother told me as a child that I was being too dramatic, like Tallulah Bankhead. I wasn't sure who that was, other than a famous dramatic actress, but based on my mother's tone of voice, it was not someone I wanted to be. I remember my own boy-child going to his room when he needed to cry. Did I send him there? What did I say? How did he hear it? I'm afraid to know those answers.

So here I was with more than 50 years of accumulated tears, living in dread of a major dam burst. It would be impossible to hold this back forever; I'd explode. So I developed strategies to control my anxiety and my tears. I began crying as much as I could at home before going out, as if to empty what was just below the surface, and collected people around me whom I could trust in case I lost control, or planned ways to get home immediately if I felt a major attack coming.

But even with careful planning, I found myself tearing up in public when I heard a song Carlton would listen to, or a young person saying "Whatever" like he used to, or when I recognized his shy smile in someone else.

I spent at least a year putting excessive stress on this leaky dam, when one Monday morning Mary Relindes Ellis, the author of *The Turtle Warrior*, visited my book club. Her book is a beautiful but painful story of abuse, war, and death. I hadn't been able to finish it before the meeting and confessed to the other women sitting in the circle that its darkness had troubled me. Several members encouraged me to keep reading, assuring me that there was redemption. I made a mental note to pick it back up when I got home.

Ms. Ellis began by telling us a little of her own chaotic family background and then she read passages from her book. She would look up periodically to connect with the audience. Once her eyes met mine. Mine immediately began their rain dance. Oh dear, I really didn't want to share my story here. I had come to hear hers. But her eyes were filling up too, as if answering mine. Neither one of us ever shed real tears; there was just a lot of watery exchange.

How could we be so connected? We were strangers. We had never met before. We didn't know each other in "real life." But here we were sitting in a circle of book lovers, sharing something truly profound. Something beyond words. After this experience could I really continue to see tears as a weakness to be ashamed of? Or could I now see them as something so intimate it can't be expressed any other way? In my lifetime of holding back, how many of these deep connections have I missed? Is this the quiet desperation Thoreau named? Am I willing to risk tears to find out? My questions continue.

Mantras

When Carlton was a young child, three sayings became his mantras. The first, "My name is Carlton," appeared when Matt, his adoptive father, tried to give him nicknames. They were silly names, Biscuit Boy and Doodle Bop, and meant to be playful. But Carlton didn't like them and would sternly remind Matt, "My name is Carlton."

I identified with that feeling. When I was a child my mother pinned a nickname on me I hated. Tuni-bell. She would use it in front of my friends and their parents. I was mortified, but my protests didn't seem to change anything. How would anyone ever take me seriously with such a stupid name?

"You're not the boss of me!" he would proclaim when he felt challenged. This declaration was usually aimed at me. I don't remember specific demands that set off this reply, although I do remember him saying it to me once in a parking lot. Did I think I was just trying to keep him away from moving cars? What did he hear? Were these his early attempts at questioning authority? What did I honestly expect from the child of a hippie chick who so regularly challenged her own mother?

The third saying appeared when he was eight. We were completing his homework ditto sheet together. A statement was given, and he was to mark an F for fact or an O for opinion in the blank before it. The challenge was to consider whether or not the statement could be proven. From this school assignment came his mantra, "That's your opinion," and it would emerge any time I was taking charge of the situation. Maybe it was his way of telling me that my all-important pronouncements might not be provable facts, or that they weren't necessarily declarations he agreed with.

These were powerful sayings. Out of the mouths of babes. They ran through my head often after he left home. It was a part of him I missed — his honest way of challenging authority in such a straightforward, childlike way.

During one long-distance conversation we had a couple years before he died, Carlton talked of being frustrated with the business world. He was hassling with car insurance and trying to get a California driver's license, and he complained of the superficiality of Hollywood. I reminded him of his mantras.

"They are your truths, Carlton. They tell you who you are."

I don't know what he heard, as I repeated his words. I was only trying to give back some of his personal wisdom.

When I was a child I had a mantra, too. "Other people have other plans," I would defiantly say to my mother when she told me how other people did things. Did I feel the need to take up for these absent "others" my mother was passing judgment on, or for myself when I didn't want to follow her way?

I sit here now with my son's mantras running through my head. "My name is Carlton." "You're not the boss of me." "That's your opinion."

Why did he leave, God?

I don't know how to answer that, Laura. What is your mantra?

"Other people have other plans."

That's your truth, sweetheart.

Leaving Home

By the time Carlton was in high school he was ready to leave home. His senior year was full of plans of going away to college, and in the fall of 1994 he left for school in Jackson, Mississippi. But it didn't turn out as he expected. He came back after a rather lackluster year, frustrated that his plans had gone so awry. He didn't volunteer much about it and because I wasn't having much success talking to either him or his father at this time, I wasn't much help. Maybe we were all hoping it would pass.

Once he moved back to Shreveport, it wasn't long before he was leaving the family home again, renting an apartment here, attending a local college and holding a couple of part-time jobs. Then came the first suicide attempt.

He moved home. Again, we didn't talk much about the situation. I asked if he wanted to talk to a therapist, and he tried one for a couple of sessions, but then wanted no more of it. He said she didn't have his experiences. I thought maybe he just wasn't sure what he was getting into. Matt has had a psychiatrist since his suicide attempt over thirty years ago, and my mother has dabbled with therapy, on and off again, for about as long. Something was not quite right about each one.

I watched and encouraged Carlton as he pursued a spring semester of college here in Shreveport with more deliberation. He talked to his professors, hoping to be more successful in their classes. He even shared some of their conversations with me. Maybe he thought education was an answer. I had certainly modeled that kind of thinking. But even the more conscientious application to his studies for a semester didn't turn out as he planned. I didn't know what else was going on in his head, and I didn't know how to ask. What did he want? I could only think to give him time and space.

Carlton lost interest in school about the time Matt moved out. I told my son he needed a full-time job if he wanted to stay at home and he returned the next evening with a job at a local department store offering medical insurance and a chance for advancement.

But a week selling ties and living with his mother wasn't what he wanted either. He quit to take a computer tech support job in Eugene, Oregon, that he found on the Internet. When I expressed concern, Carlton didn't want to talk about it. He needed to leave again.

This dear young man worked so hard at finding his place. Initial results from conventional avenues only caused him frustration. All I knew to do at that time was get out of the way and let him keep trying. So early one February morning in 1998, I hugged him hard at the kitchen door and tearfully watched his packed car pull out of the driveway. He called every night from the road, recounting his day and mapping out the next. But once he was in Eugene, all I received was an e-mail with his phone number and address and for the next year-and-a-half, he didn't answer any phone calls or e-mails. I told myself that what he needed was a chance to be on his own to learn his path, so I "worked" at learning mine.

Then one day in the summer of 1999, he called to tell me that he was moving to Hollywood, California, with a friend, and I began hearing from him every few months. He still didn't answer calls or e-mails, but I was grateful when he initiated the connection. It sounded like he was finding what he wanted, and I was able to let go of more worry. He came home only twice — Christmas 1999 and the 2001 family reunion. I tried not to overwhelm him while he was here, despite being anxious to know how his life was unfolding. In hindsight, maybe the busyness and distractions of Christmas and the family reunion kept me from being as available to him as I, his mother, could have been.

Oh dear. My mind spun as I retraced these events in his abbreviated life and my part in them, wishing I could change them, live them over, and make different choices. I turned to my pen.

What was he looking for? What was it he wanted that he couldn't find here? What more should I have done? Why did he encourage me to leave? Could he see something holding me back here, too?

I don't know. Why are you still here?

I tried to leave. I wanted the darkness to swallow me, too. I was so scared.

So why are you still here?

Unfinished business keeps me here. The flickering light my pen scribbles toward. Whoever you are in my journal talking to me, teaching me how to take care of myself.

And what have you learned?

How to identify what is going on around me and how to put my feelings into words, so I can look at them more honestly and learn from them without becoming too overwhelmed.

On the Trail to Oregon

My 79-year-old mother's 88-year-old sister Jo lives on the coast of Oregon, but the numerous breaks in her osteoporotic bones prevented her from traveling. Her 90-year-old husband Ralph died in the spring of 2004. The only way Mother could visit her involved a flight change in the sprawling Dallas airport.

It seemed the two would not be able to get together. Mother talked about it a lot. She said she wasn't sure she wanted to go, but continued to talk about it. My urge to seize the day rather than live with regret pushed me to offer to accompany her. She hesitated and counter-offered with excuses and conditions, but after a little time and compromise, a plan was set for ten days near Waldport, Oregon, at the end of October, 2004.

I considered what this might mean for me. I wanted to see the ocean and my Auntie Jo again, and I was hungry for more family information from a primary source. I wanted to know what it meant to be a Mechlin woman. My mother and I shared a long and difficult relationship, constantly pushing against each other to be who we wanted to be. I wanted to know more about what that struggle meant. I wanted to learn all I could about mothers and their children.

The Dallas airport was our first real challenge and I was grateful to have Mother as an excuse to ride the little cart from Delta gate 1A to gate 37. We landed in Portland without a problem, but the drive from Portland to Waldport, using my cousin's car and e-mailed directions, along with Mother's insistent navigation, was very tiresome. When I followed the highway according to my cousin's instructions, she adamantly told me this was not the way Uncle Ralph went. Were there two correct ways, I wondered? Did it matter?

Let it go, Laura, I told myself, stepping on the accelerator to speed up this part of the journey. It was much too early in the trip to tangle. We went Uncle Ralph's way, so she began worrying aloud about what I had eaten for breakfast.

I packed books and notebooks in preparation for this trip and planned walks on the beach and side trips into town as additional outlets. My aunt has a wonderful live-in sitter Ron who treated all three of us like queens, a job I originally feared I might be responsible for.

My poet uncle's writing group met at their house one day, and I bravely read the story "The Phone Call" for my first audience. A few days later I took a day trip alone into Newport to peruse an eclectic bookstore crammed with new and used books, and made a bracelet in a shop devoted entirely to beads. Throughout the week my aunt and uncle's collection of friends stopped by for stimulating conversations on the state of the world. I volunteered at a literacy center run by my aunt's friend, where a nine-year-old girl and I took turns reading to each other. One evening Mom, Aunt Jo, the sitter and I went to the Newport community theater to see a local production of *Cabaret,* and I sat between two women very much in love with the arts. I found myself participating as so much more than a daughter and niece. I was a Mechlin woman.

However, the older women continued to give me constant unsolicited advice and "constructive criticism" and call me "Lolly," another of my childhood names. But I practiced overriding the frustration in my head for a later session with my notebook.

Nevertheless, the last full day we were there, a fight was building inside me that I feared I would not be able to contain. I didn't want to end such an enlightening trip by slipping into twelve-year-old behavior, and thus fulfilling a possible expectation. I left the house to walk in a light rain (without the suggested umbrella) to the beach. Arriving at the water's edge, I sat down on a driftwood log and cried. But within a few minutes I was standing, yelling into the ocean. "My name is not Lolly. I am not twelve years old." The ocean roared back. I repeated my cry and the ocean again responded. Back and forth we screamed until my tears were drained. The clouds broke, the sun shone through and, to the south towards land, a rainbow arced across the sky.

When I told my cousin Nancy Jo about it in a long-distance phone call later that day, she said, "Oh, that's God answering, 'And this is my daughter in whom I am well pleased.'"

I liked the way this generation of Mechlin women interprets that experience.

Mothering

For several years after Carlton's death I obsessively reviewed his life, desperately trying to figure out where I went so wrong. What was the glaring error that shut him down at the age of 27?

I mothered the best way I knew how. Advice from Dr. Spock, the leading expert at the time, was assimilated as well as my college-graduate self could understand it. I was particularly fluent in colic, leaning heavily on Spock's support through Carlton's restless nights.

His dad moved out when Carlton was four months old. We had married soon after his commitment to the Army was finished. Maybe the challenge of both fatherhood and husbandhood was more than he signed up for. Although my friends assured me he would change his mind as soon as he saw the baby, it didn't happen, and my independent self took over.

Carlton was six months old when we moved back to Shreveport to live with my parents, where I learned first-hand what support I appreciated from them (rest from the demands of mothering) and what I preferred to do for myself (feeding schedules and the need for daycare). It was time to find a place for just the two of us. The newly-liberated woman-self needed some rooms of her own.

When Carlton was in second grade, I took a sabbatical and we went to Austin, Texas, so I could pursue a doctorate in education. But by the next summer, following my advancement to candidacy, the title I chose instead was wife. Maybe I thought what we really needed was a man around the house.

I sent Carlton to the best daycares and magnet schools, enrolled him in t-ball and soccer, and celebrated his birthday parties at McDonald's and the skating rink. He earned his black belt in *tae kwon do*, was the head chorister in the Shreveport Boychoir, and played on many baseball teams along the way. I did what I thought other mothers were doing, pushing ourselves and our children, trying to fit in.

When he became a less-than-conscientious student in the seventh grade, I relied on my experience as a middle school teacher. I helped him get organized then held him accountable for his own unstable grades. The teacher/mother self appeared.

In high school he pulled away, becoming moody and uncommunicative. I remembered a similar feeling from my own high school days. Because I had wanted more separation from my family, I tried to allow his struggle. I searched for ways to put up my own boundaries and respect his, but I was experiencing challenges with my husband at this time, too. I obviously needed some separation from the demands of my style of mothering the people in this house.

When Carlton went off to college I gave him my blessing. When he came home, I welcomed him back. When he wanted his own apartment, I balked, trying to explain the expenses of such an adventure, then reluctantly released him. After his first suicide attempt, I welcomed him home again to regain his footing in a safe place because I thought that was what I would want. I tried talking with him, but received only evasive answers. When he left for the West Coast, all I knew to do was to let him go because I knew I still wanted my own release, too.

I mothered the best I knew how through the different stages in my own life. I related to him the way I thought he might have wanted, but I realize now that it was the way I wanted to be mothered. Maybe Carlton was trying to tell me that. It was certainly what I was trying to tell my mom.

And now, with no biological child on Earth to mother, I sit here with myself — my other child, the one I've been wanting a mother for all my life. Mama Laura needed to know how to take care of little Laura, and the pen has served as family counselor while we learned how to communicate. We watched closely as it scribbled our scariest fears and most passionate desires into the notebook. We saw our deepest thoughts, the ones we haven't been able to share with anyone else. And we talked to each other as only someone with this kind of intimate information could, telling in our most intimate and honest way that we are safe and loved.

Mr. Know-it-All and the Mystery Man

There was often a debate raging in my head between Mr. Know-it-All and the Mystery Man. My left side (rational thinking), so heavily relied upon in the past, fights with my right side (creative thinking) which yearns for release but fears losing control.

I would replay a phone call over and over in my head, considering all the layers of possible meanings and wondering which to follow, amazed at the different facets of simple conversation and how they paralleled other events. Was life supposed to be this complicated?

Complexities can be stimulating to a thinking person, but nothing went unexamined. A movie, a song, a news story, a chance encounter, a casual phrase, all got the third degree in my overactive mind, as I tried to piece together how everything related. I had to limit daily activities just to have enough time to process.

Brainstorming was what we called it in my classroom. I would stand in front of the blackboard listing the students' ideas as fast as they called them out. But I longed for a little less chaotic weather inside my own head.

I wanted more proof of a web of life and the interconnectedness to all beings. Why couldn't I just let it go and enjoy being? Must everything be a puzzle needing to be solved?

One morning I found myself on another quest. Dostoevsky's novel, *The Brothers Karamazov*, was Carlton's favorite. *Crime and Punishment* had been one of mine as a young adult. I saw this as an important link and immediately wanted more information. I went to the Internet to research Fyodor Dostoevsky and found that he had had seizures and with these seizures, visions. His book *The Idiot* describes them. Oh dear. Did Carlton's childhood seizures offer him insights? The first one happened when he was a toddler and was fever-related. But the second one, when he was seven, was never medically explained. He took phenobarbital for a year and had no more grand mal episodes. I wanted more information and made a mental note to read *The Idiot*.

Then there was his first suicide attempt. Was it a near-death experience and another possible vision? We didn't talk about that. Did he discuss it with anyone?

Could that have helped? I thought of the people I could have put him in touch with, if only I had known. OK, this spinning was not productive thinking, I rationalized.

But that didn't stop me.

I had suffered migraines when Carlton was young and remembered the auras that preceded them, warning me of the pain to follow. Was this some concentrated sensory awareness trying to get my attention? I don't know, and I don't have migraines any more. But within the first few months after his death, I had dreams of light. Were these significant? Should I analyze them further? So many pieces, so little time.

My mind continued its spinning routine, stirring up more questions than answers, and I anxiously wanted a bottom line. But the harder Mr.-Know-it-All worked at making everything fit, the less certain I felt about anything.

I didn't have time to write in my journal before a friend and I went out one evening to listen to music. Because it had been such an intense day I was afraid I might not be good company in such a fragmented state. But we went to a blues jam in a dark, smoky club full of people grooving on the sights and sounds, far away from my spinning light. No one there was the least bit interested in Mr.-Know-it-All's research.

Ah, I reasoned, smiling at the unexpected outcome. Mystery Man showed up with the perfect solution to my unsolvable problem. Let it go and enjoy the present.

Magical Child

I first met Caitlin, an outgoing lovable five-year-old, at my church in 1998. She showed up in my life just before Carlton left for the West Coast. We immediately adopted each other, she becoming little Laura and I her second mama. We'd sit together on the pew, singing hymns, writing notes, and drawing pictures on church bulletins. On Christmas Eve she sat with me as family, for my own didn't attend.

We had little contact during the week. I went to one of her elementary school basketball games; she came to my house once to play with the classroom animals I kept during the summer. And we exchanged presents. An angel necklace for her. An angel picture frame for me. But by the time she had finished second grade, I left that church and lost my weekly contact with Caitlin.

On January 19, 2003, she showed up in my life again, this time at my house for the family visitation following Carlton's death. She brought me a big hug and soft stuffed puppy who looked amazingly like Princess. I held tightly to that comforting toy for the rest of the day, grateful for the reconnection. I didn't see her again for nearly two years.

I learned she was dancing the role of Clara in the 2004 Christmas production of *The Nutcracker*, when my niece Laura Beth played a soldier. Naturally I planned on going, but several weeks before the scheduled December performance, the nearby branch library offered excerpts to the public. Laura Beth wouldn't be dancing, but Caitlin definitely would. I picked a bouquet of tiny, fragrant sweetheart roses from my backyard, packed my disposable camera, and drove to the library, eager to connect with her again.

I was standing in the back of the room when she skipped out, adorned in golden ringlets and a red velvet pinafore. My arms wrapped around me in my own big hug as I watched this beautiful, graceful seventh grader dance around the room.

I became Clara-Caitlin, the magical child. I thought of what I remembered of that age. Seventh grade seemed anything but enchanting for me. I had moved from the safety of an elementary school I attended for six years with most of the same friends and classmates to the overwhelming challenge of junior high with so many new faces, changing classes with tardy bells in between, dressing out in gym, and open seating in the lunchroom. Yet here I was, on a November night at the library I claimed as one of my safe places, reborn as a confident dancing beauty.

I haven't followed Caitlin's Sunday-to-Sunday life as she grows into the woman she'll become, and I have missed her. She's another child I was once very attached to. But her dance back into my life on a late fall evening reassured me of our sacred bond, the magical child we both carry within us. She has helped me understand Viktor Frankl's words, "love loved is never lost."

On my refrigerator is a picture taken that night after the performance. Caitlin and I are standing together smiling and holding onto each other in the children's section of this branch library. A bulletin board behind us reads, "Believe in the Magic."

Heaven

I never had to think so seriously about heaven before. My childhood image of angels sitting on clouds playing harps wasn't working.

What really happens when we die? Where do we go? What happened to my son, the child I used to call Angel Baby? His life was just getting started. Where is he? Does he have friends? Is he happy? Did he know something about his choices that I don't know? Is where he is now preferable to where he was?

Lying still, listening, I can feel his presence. Pictures of his life run through my head, flickering and clicking like the old 16mm film projector from my own elementary school days. He is as close as my beating heart and as present as my thoughts. What is heaven? Where do all the souls go when they've finished here on earth?

His ashes, the last tangible part of his earthly form, lay scattered on the forest floor at Caddo Lake Nature Trail near Uncertain, Texas. The picture of him resting in a place that renews itself naturally with the seasons was reassuring to my organic gardener's mind.

I saw Carlton as a small child holding hands with Kristi, his best friend when he was a toddler. She died of a seizure several years before Carlton, and left behind a toddler son. Are they holding hands now?

When Carlton was in seventh grade we got a dog named Cody, a stray hit by a car and rescued by a friend. Several years before Carlton died, the dog became anxious and disoriented, and I had to put him to sleep. Our vet said he was worn out from such a full life. Have Carlton and Cody found relief together?

There was Lonnie Bell, my friend Linda's mother, who died ten days after Carlton did. She knew him when he was a little boy and watched him grow up. Is she playing grandmother to my child now?

Is he with Patrick, a Cub Scout friend full of potential, who died suddenly as a young adult when he unknowingly ate seafood, to which he was allergic? Are they in a heavenly Scout hut working on arrow points together?

Is he at the baseball game he alludes to in the dream? A week before Carlton's freshman year in high school, Kevin, a graduate of the school and a baseball star about to begin his major league career, was killed in a car wreck. Is Carlton playing ball in a league with Kevin?

Has he met Jennifer, a college freshman who was tragically killed one night about a month after Carlton died when some guys were fooling around with a gun? Carlton didn't know her, but I once taught next door to her mother. Are they comparing notes on what it's like to be the teacher's kid?

The Columbia shuttle blew up upon reentry several weeks after Carlton's death. Seven astronauts were sent to their fiery deaths. My poet uncle compared this event to a Viking funeral. Has my own Muse found his place with them?

Has he had a chance to talk to Dostoevsky or Einstein or Shakespeare or Alexander Dumas? Or the author of the *Gospel of Thomas?* Carlton's collection of books told me he would recognize their voices.

The day after Christmas, 2004, the tsunami hit, killing hundreds of thousands of people. We wrung our hands and tried to find someone to blame for such a tragedy. I watched, detached, not feeling the grief such a disaster should trigger. With Carlton's help I had my most reassuring image of heaven so far. He was up "there" with his big kind eyes and sweet shy smile, helping welcome all of those scared children as they signed in at the pearly gates. He was like an orientation counselor or a big brother at camp or college. He knew just what to say, how to help them settle in to their new surroundings and feel right at home, like I'm sure others did for him. It was now his turn to be the guide and introduce these new angels to some old friends of his.

Renewed Energy

Anniversaries

There are six weeks of anniversaries that fall between November 28, Carlton's birthday, and January 11, the day he died. The first year I carefully planned how and where I would spend my time. I went to Biloxi for his birthday and Thanksgiving, and quietly celebrated my own birthday on December 5th with friends. For Christmas the family had a traditional dinner at my brother Bruce's house, and I gave everyone a little notebook and pen, inviting them into my world to tell their own story. On January 11, I stayed alone with my notebook, letting the answering machine take outside calls.

But after that first anniversary in 2003, a new family event was added. January 15, 2004, was the day my brothers and I took Dad to the War Veterans Home in Monroe.

So, on the second year of anniversaries, as autumn fell into winter, I needed a new plan. On the trip to Oregon in October I had successfully read "The Phone

Call." Then when I traveled to Boulder, Colorado, in mid-November to meet with my writing group, I read the story again. It was, however, the only one I had been able to write. Everything else was still journaling. I wanted to turn the whole experience into a story to share with others, but I wasn't sure how to do it.

So I did what I knew how to do best. I continued to let my pen scribble in my composition book until I had a clearer idea. Day after day, page after page, I held tightly to that pen as I swam through murky words and bled all over the pages, desperately looking for relief. I ventured out only for groceries, a visit to Stoner Hill, the meetings with teacher friends on Fridays, or The Trapped Truth Society, my local writers' group, on Sundays.

> *I tell people my pen is saving me,*
> *but I'm not sure what that means.*

> **Keep writing.**

The second year I decided to celebrate Carlton's birthday, Thanksgiving, and my birthday alone. On Christmas, weary from the silence, but not ready for my own entangling family, I went to Linda's house for Christmas dinner with her two daughters, their husbands, and five children. It was an invitation a friend as close as Linda knew to offer.

> *I'm still writing, but I need a plan.*

> **It's time to read your journals,**
> **Laura. You've poured your soul**

*into two years of composition
books. Read what you wrote.*

Well, I had read the first two, and parts of others, and I read as I continued journaling. I thought I could just lift little sections from the books to tell my story, but I had a hard time finding excerpts that made sense out of context.

So I began with the intention of reading a notebook a day, looking for something more than witty little phrases or insights. Settling on the sofa with a stack of journals on the floor beside me, I opened the first one. After four days and four journals, I had to put the plan aside just to catch my breath.

*Who is telling this story? How did
she get inside my pen? How does she
know all this stuff?*

Laura, Jake, Buddy, Mom, Dad,
Bruce, Avery, Laura Beth

It's you, dear. Has been all along. Patiently waiting inside to be invited out.

The more I read, the more I knew my story was not just clever little sections to be lifted from journals. A significant person or idea would make a brief appearance on one page, but then wouldn't return again for another journal or two. I needed time and distance to see this unfolding as my pen connected the dots.

I began reading the next composition book, and my pen jotted down two- or three-word phrases on little scraps of paper. I continued to read and more phrases emerged. After several days of this "note-taking," I wanted to explore the phenomenon further. Choosing the phrase "Avery" and using Natalie Goldberg's method, I did a ten-minute writing on it. The pen told the story of my niece, start to finish, in the allotted time. Amazed, I tried the topic, "A Safe Place," and again the pen began its timed dance, describing my circle of teacher friends. Maybe this was not a fluke. Maybe this really was something bigger than myself. Maybe my pen really has been my salvation.

The second anniversary of events had something new to celebrate. The gift of my pen: how it recorded what was happening around me and inside me, showing me in my own handwriting who I am and from where I had come.

A Conversation with my Pen

One morning soon after this awareness, I woke with an amazing thought. This day could be as magnificent as I wanted it to be. Any discomfort or fear was my own choice. Had I still not given myself permission to be fully present? Did I still think I didn't "deserve" it? Was I still reviewing that third-grade report card that told me I wasn't yet good enough with multiplication facts? My pen eagerly joined the discussion.

> **Well, Laura, that's why you were in the third grade. That's exactly where you were supposed to be to learn them.**

> Oh. So everywhere I am is where I'm "supposed" to be. What I need to learn is right in front of me?

> **Yep. All you need is eyes to see and ears to hear.**

> Here I sit on my blue-flowered sofa in the middle of my living room with my fluffy Princess dog stretched across my lap. What does that mean?

> **What do you want it to mean?**

> That this is where I'm supposed to be, in a comfortable place with a

loving companion and a pen that talks to me as my most intimate friend.

So enjoy it.

But what if I get bored? What if I'm ready to leave this safety and go explore?

And your problem with that is...

Well, I might get scared. I might get too far into the adventure and panic.

Laura, you have such an active imagination. How do you calm yourself back down? How do you get through the fear?

I talk to you.

Bingo. We writers need active imaginations. If we just sit in our living rooms on blue-flowered sofas with fluffy dogs in our laps and intimate pens in our hands, we get bored. We need to get out and have a little adventure every now and then, so we'll have something interesting to write about.

That makes sense.

Now I'm back with the Laura I recognize, the one who makes sure she doesn't get too far into the adventure without having a way to get back.

So. I need the creative Laura to take a few risks and the rational Laura to live to tell about it?

Sure, if that's the way you want to see it.

RELEASING the LIGHT

Light Visions

One night after those first dark months following Carlton's death I had several dreams about light. When I woke in the morning I wanted to paint them rather than write about them. So I took copy paper from my computer printer tray, a yellow plastic box of watercolors, and a little cup of water to the safety of my sofa to explore this new idea. With a brush full of re-hydrated color, I touched the paper. Blurry images appeared. I watched as the paintbrush danced like my pen. The only words I could write on these pages full of watery color were titles.

The first image I painted was a little gray stick person. She must be a girl because she had on a dress. Her body was being unzipped from the head down. A splash of yellow watercolor emerged from the open top of her head, moving up to the left-hand corner of the page. With my pen I wrote in the bottom right-hand corner, "Releasing the Light."

A little gray stick figure was standing alone in the next picture. This time it was not obviously a girl. There was no dress. There was, however, a gray question mark directly over his/her head. Above this mark to one side was a gray spotlight emitting yellow light. On the other side of the question mark was a yellow dollar sign. In the right corner of this page, I wrote "Fame and Fortune: the Artificial Light."

Another picture contained more than a dozen gray stick people. They were limply drifting up the page to the splash of yellow color on the left side. I called this picture "Going Toward the Light."

GOING TOWARD the LIGHT

The fourth one had a small androgynous gray figure being pulled toward the yellow light with the word "words" printed over and over and falling from the bottom half of the figure. There was no title for this page.

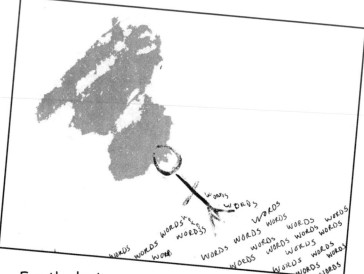

For the last picture I used a different color from my paint box. Along the bottom of the page with a wide sweep I left a trail of brown "ground" with black-ink arrows pointing downward through it. Along the top of the page was a band of yellow "light" with arrows pointing upward. In the middle there were four gray figures in progressive stances. The first one was standing upright on the brown color. The second was tilted slightly and rising above the "ground," and the third one leaned over even more, rising farther from the

brown

slash. Finally, the fourth one, in a prone position, was halfway between the yellow above and the brown below. The caption on this watercolor asked, "Why Walk When You Can Fly?"

I didn't consciously set this up. I think I was only responding from my experience catalog I call dreams. Each picture contained the yellow light image and the gray "person" image. The first one showed yellow breaking open from the gray body to join the larger light. Was this me trying to follow Carlton? Was the second one, depicting confusion over the lights, representing the challenges of living on Earth? The third, appearing as if a universal force pulled all of us toward the greater yellow light. Was this the "perfect team" the raspy Carlton-voice alluded to in my earlier dream? And the picture with "words" falling from the little gray figure as it ascended to the light? Was it telling me that words are needed here for communication, and not in the Great Light? Was this about my job on Earth as storyteller? The last picture's caption, "Why Walk When You Can Fly?" is the title of a favorite song by Mary Chapin Carpenter and has been a guiding light through my meandering search.

The figure was flying parallel to Earth and sky, letting her heart and soul guide her, rising above the distractions on earth. In the world, but not of the world. In the word, but not of the word.

Was the yellow light God? Love? My Carlton connection? Was it the inspiration I needed to keep me focused on my work here? And the brown in the last picture. To remind me to stay grounded? To stay present and aware of where I am?

I considered the dream I had when Carlton talked to me. It must have come from the same "place" of stored images and thoughts. The universal stream encouraging me to trust my unfolding. The assurance of a force that continues to unite us. A promise that I'm not alone and never have been. What my "child" and I have been looking for.

I will continue to listen to my dreams, knowing they are one way God talks to me, as I daily choose the best ways to stay connected to the world

Abstaining from Whine

The first audience to hear my story "The Phone Call" was my uncle's writing group in Oregon. It was a group of people I might never see again, so I decided it could be a safe place to share something this personal. We took turns reading our offerings as we sat in a circle in my aunt's living room, a view of the Pacific Ocean in the background. Several writers received immediate, encouraging feedback. They were told whose writing it sounded like or where it might be submitted for publication. I was feeling comfortable with this group. I could do this. So when it was my turn, I read my story with a voice that broke only once, near the end. When I finished the room was very quiet. I wasn't hearing the feedback I had expected. The only comment I remember was from a man who told me his sister had a child who died. I wasn't sure what that response meant. I sat still, waiting. Soon the next reader began. I felt like I was underwater with muffled noises swirling around me. I couldn't understand what was happening. After the readings, a man walked up to me and told me he was a psychologist. I needed that voice. I could hear those words and was back again in my aunt's living room.

The next day a retired architect from the group told me he liked my writing because it wasn't whiney. I heard that as feedback I had expected, and it felt good. My rational brain began to process it. He named a behavior I wished to display in public, while I searched for relief from this overwhelming fear and accepted my experience as an opportunity for growth.

But just because my writing didn't sound whiney didn't mean I was abstaining from the childish behavior. To declare that I didn't spend a lot of time fighting it, or getting really angry at God, or feeling close to giving up would be an outright lie. Almost every morning for the first two years I would lie in bed, stare at the ceiling, and consider what I might be able to accomplish during the day. Then I would have to make an intentional decision to get up. Every night, again in the same position, I spent time deliberately letting go of the day's accumulation of fears, shame, and regrets so that I could get to sleep. But these holding-on and letting-go sessions were not just limited to my bedroom. I found myself making them over and over throughout the day, everywhere I went.

I admit to screaming, slamming doors, and throwing pillows and books inside the house. Princess, the albino dove, and these walls have all witnessed this unruly behavior. I'm not sure what I have said during these tantrums, but I'm quite sure it wasn't "nice." OK, I could be a very angry child.

At night I cried long and hard into my pillow. *It's not fair, God,* I choked. *I've tried so hard to be good, to do what I thought I was supposed to do, and this is the thanks I get?* Well, that certainly sounded whiney by most standards.

But I worked hard to keep this fussy child to myself. I didn't think anyone else should have to deal with her. After all, I was a grown-up and should act like one, at least in the presence of others. So I spent much time alone with my notebook, afraid of unleashing my monster child on some innocent bystander.

In the first months following Carlton's death, when I was so agitated, the writing in my journal should have produced enough heat to start fires. But two years later as I read these journals, I saw fierce rantings for sure, but there was something else. Calm, rational words were woven in between the rage, showing me other perspectives. How could they come from the same pen?

Often by mid-afternoon the living room began to close in on me. My internal energy was depleted. I was tired of sitting still on a sofa with my notebook because I was afraid of disturbing the world. My pen identified this feeling and suggested a walk in the park, or a movie, or a library visit, or a get-together with safe friends. I was taking care of the lonely child. This extension beyond the sofa reminded me that I *did* want to be with others again.

I needed this compass from within. Something that knew how to take care of me when everyone else was busy with their own whiney selves. I needed to be able to hear the nurturing mother-voice who whispered those loving words through her pen.

No, I am not "cured." I guess this is probably all part of the process. As hard as I try, I can't seem to completely abstain from my childish behaviors, and there are still panicky times when I'm afraid I'll cause too much damage. I try to listen to those who can help best — God, me, and my mother nature.

Doing Research

A new friend showed up in my life as I was becoming comfortable in this adventure called writing. Actually she was not "new." Scotty is two years younger than I and was in my brother's third-grade class. On a spring Sunday afternoon in 2002, about six months before Carlton died, she attended the weekly Trapped Truth Society reading. We recognized each other from the past and immediately reconnected.

She, coming off a messy divorce, and with two young teenagers, had picked up writing again, having been a journalist earlier in her adult career. The stories she shared on Sundays were about chaotic relationships. My offerings at this time were anecdotes from my teaching experience. With Scotty, Lee (an African-American man who wrote about growing up in rural Louisiana with 13 brothers and sisters), and me, what was once a writer's group of poets was now being challenged by our prosaic ways.

Scotty was a great affirmer of my novice attempts at writing and I, having already experienced my own messy divorce and the raising of a teenager, offered some proof that she too could survive.

But when Carlton died in January 2003, our relationship changed. We began sharing concerns about the expectations of mothering and our roles in the family, and wondered with frustration how we were supposed to be everything to everybody. We exchanged notes on the research we had done on our own, lending encouragement to each other.

We began spending more than Sunday afternoons together. She was more outgoing, and I needed help reentering the world. We went to hear my brothers' band and her friend's band, which landed us in casino lounges, biker bars, and singles dances. Not a problem, we thought, with an air of detachment. We writers were here to observe the human animal. We were merely doing research.

We also went to several art openings at her friend's gallery, where we sipped wine, nibbled cheese and crackers, and studied the newest exhibits. We had favorites, and they were not necessarily the same. I struggled to articulate why I liked the simple big red barn better than the swirling acrylic moon pictures she chose. Another creative friend dubbed us the "Art

Divas," a name we modestly accepted. After all, it *was* for the sake of research.

Scotty and I exchanged new "other worldly" ideas, testing the reaction of the other as we gave voice to our inner thoughts. We discussed our dreams, spirituality, Kabbalah, and channeling, even though we didn't really know what we were talking about. We were trying to find words to connect to something too elusive to pin down. Again, it was where the research was leading us.

We compared families and growing up in the same white middle-class Shreveport neighborhood in the '50s and '60s and found we shared similar secrets and questions, harbored through the decades. We wondered about others in this setting who may have these same hidden stories, and how we might find out.

Everyone should have a "Scotty" friend, an honest, trustworthy reflection of where you are and what you're thinking, a person outside yourself to offer support and encouragement through the scarier parts of the journey.

We did it creatively, assuming the roles of writers when we needed to, and witnessing growth in ourselves and each other. Who knows? Maybe it really was research for the sake of our art.

Dancing at Weddings

The dancing started at Allison's wedding, her second marriage after a traumatic first one, and all her friends were there to celebrate. Because it was on July 3rd, we sent the happy couple off under an arc of lit sparklers at the end of the reception. But for me the real celebration happened before the fireworks. A local country western band began playing the traditional daddy/daughter dance. A few couples then moved to the floor, followed by several little girls in swirling party dresses.

Children naturally dance when they hear music. They haven't yet learned restraint. I remember a young Carlton dancing with abandon and rolling on the grassy hillside of the outdoor festival's amphitheater where his uncles' band played. He was so full of life.

As I watched these dancers at the wedding on the shiny hardwood floor, my body began moving to the music's rhythm. But I held back; I had no partner. I concentrated on Martha and Al circling the floor and the little girls twirling and spinning, while I waltzed in my head. A few minutes of this mental dancing, however, wasn't enough. I stood up and began moving around the table where my friends were sitting. It was not exactly a dance, more a continuation of the rhythmic swaying that had been going on inside me. My swaying around the table and Martha and Al's dancing merged and we moved onto the floor. Once out there, I saw other women in groups. Some of my friends joined me and the other women, and our individual expressions connected into one big circle. The frolicking children tumbled into the middle of it. It was so full of joy.

The next wedding I attended was for Mary Margaret's son James. At the church I watched three of Carlton's childhood friends serve as groomsmen and swallowed the ache in my throat as I wished for my notebook. But the reception with a disc jockey soon followed, and I was ready to dance again. First there was a mother/son dance, then a father/daughter one. As I waited my turn, I began that moving-around-the-tables thing again. A young groomsman I didn't know asked me to dance, an idea a friend had set into motion. He was very polite and talked about his mother. This time there was no women's circle or dancing children, and after several couple dances, the younger guests took over the dance floor. The bride Danielle, hiking her wedding dress up to her knees, led the young women in a line dance. I recognized it as one I had learned on my cruise. This was the opening I had been watching for, and with Allan, the groom's father, encouraging me I was out on the floor in line with the younger women.

The next wedding was Mary Margaret and Allan's other son, Allan, Jr. It was in Dallas, so several of the

Steel Magnolias decided to make a road trip. I eagerly packed my dancing shoes, wondering how this one would work.

It was an elegant wedding in a traditionally ornate church, which was a bit unnerving for me, and there were many more strangers there than at the last two. At the fashionable hotel reception, a twelve-piece band began playing. My body started moving again. But this time I planted myself firmly in the upholstered seat, intent on acting like a grown-up. Maybe I wouldn't dance this time, I sighed, and mentally began journaling about it. But while the band was on break, Shanan, the bride, came over to the circular table where her new mother-in-law's friends were sitting. She sat with us for a while, then still talking, got up and moved us to the dance floor. Soon several middle-aged women, Shanan, and her friends were swaying together to a recording of Abba's "Dancing Queen." It was perfect.

Dancing is a way of celebrating, letting go and giving in to the universal rhythm that moves our world. I want to be a part of that celebration, and weddings are appropriate places to join forces. Maybe this is a place where women and children can lead.

Valentine's Day

Oh dear. It's time for another national celebration of coupling and I'm busy wrestling

with a concept of wholeness within myself.
What if I don't get any valentines? I guess this
is another holdover from third grade. How can I
creatively address this Valentine's Day phobia?
I've still got two days. I can send myself a card.

I went into my spare bedroom/junk room for
watercolors and paper, then settled on the living room
sofa for inspiration. First I painted a big red heart in
the middle of a page torn from my sketch pad, added
a stylized splash of color in each corner, representing
flowers. I smiled as I admired my creation. With a
black Sharpie pen I wrote "I love..." in the middle of
the heart and proceeded to list traits I love about
myself all around it. "Your sense of humor," "your
tenacity," "your smile," "your compassion." I was a bit
tentative at first. After all, I have had fifty years of
being told "humility" was a virtue. Of course, I thought,
and added "your humility" to the attributes.

I grew bolder and the page filled. This valentine was
for my eyes only; I didn't need to explain it to anyone
else. When it was covered with words and color, I
slipped the paper into a large self-addressed manila
envelope, added an extra stamp to prevent something
as tacky as insufficient postage, then drove to the
post office to drop it in the outside mailbox. I felt an
immediate surge, thinking of the special valentine I
could look forward to.

Monday the 14th came. I went to my book club
meeting and the Head Queen of the Pulpwood Queens

began by passing out pink Mardi Gras beads and rhinestone pins for everyone. I put on my new jewels in celebration.

After the meeting I drove across town to pick up Princess where she had been boarded over the weekend. As she was handed to me, I received the kind of Valentine love only a tail-wagging, sloppy-kissing, fluffy friend could give.

By the time we got back home, the mailbox was holding two cards for me — one from a cousin and one from a new friend in Oregon — and a rejection form letter from a publishing house. But the big envelope with my homemade valentine was not there. I was consoling myself with the thought that at least I would have mail again on the 15th when the mailman walked up to hand-deliver it.

That evening I attended a community education forum. The crowd was smaller than usual, perhaps because of the holiday. But sandwiches, chips and cookies were laid out for the participants. A Valentine dinner, I mused, and helped myself to the spread. I mentally added this offering, along with the gathering of compatible people full of stimulating conversation and a shared vision, to my growing list of valentines.

As we left, the forum coordinator handed each of us two long-stemmed red carnations. Flowers, too! I'm not sure I could have imagined a more loving day, even if I had planned it myself.

God's Plan

February 28, 2005, was Dad's 90th birthday and I felt it should be special. The whole family hadn't assembled in one place since Christmas dinner in 2003 at my brother Bruce's house, and my father now lived a hundred miles away at a nursing home.

I assumed several plans were being considered as each participant played with his or her own idea of how the patriarch's special day could be celebrated. Once upon a time, as the big sister and assistant mother of this family, I thought it was my responsibility to be in charge of such an important event. I wasn't so sure anymore.

Buddy was to play solo acoustical guitar on Friday the 25th in Monroe. That's great, I noted. He would already be there and the rest of us could drive over Saturday morning. I volunteered to bring Mom and the grandchildren.

Bruce had an appointment with the financial director of the nursing home on Friday. This was to be the director's last day and there was a lot of unfinished business over Dad's Army pension. It seemed logical to me that Bruce would stay overnight in Monroe and join us in a Saturday morning party. But that didn't seem to be Bruce's plan. He thought he might just see Dad that evening after his meeting and then come home.

The celebration wasn't unfolding the way I imagined, which could be a real challenge for me. But I was trying to take less responsibility for other family members' lives and actions. I could still take Mom, the grandkids, and a cake over there, like I volunteered. If that was all we had, that would be enough. At this point I wasn't even sure Bud's idea was to meet us at the nursing home on Saturday morning.

Friday came and Bud called me before heading east to Monroe. He would spend the night at a motel there and be at the nursing home in the morning for the party. I asked if he would bring his guitar, assuming that was something he had already planned.

"I haven't even thought of that," he replied, agreeing to the idea.

Two hours later, Bruce called from Interstate 20, thirty minutes west of Monroe, to tell me the social worker just told him the finance director didn't come in on Fridays. My brother turned the car around in frustration, returning to Shreveport. But later that day, when he was back home, the finance director called, asking where he was. It was an obvious miscommunication. They rescheduled a meeting for Saturday morning. When Bruce called to report this new development to me, I envisioned a party coming together after all, but quickly picked up my notebook to write rather than talk about it, so it would "just happen."

Early Saturday morning the younger grandchildren's mother dropped Jake and Laura Beth at my house. Avery the teenager was driving her own car so she could stop to spend the night with friends at the college she would be attending that summer. I was to take the kids, a bakery German chocolate cake, a two-liter bottle of root beer, and paper plates and cups to Bruce's house, where we would get into his Voyager minivan, stop by Mother's house to pick her up, and then drive the hundred miles to Monroe. Bud would show up with his guitar at the nursing home after he woke up.

Once at the home, the social worker offered us a private meeting room, and behind closed doors we became the magical Flett family again. Bruce and I climbed on top of one of the tables to demonstrate the line dance to "Sentimental Journey" the way our third grade teacher had taught us. Jake, Bruce's son, eagerly joined in on top of his own table, as Bud picked out guitar chords and Avery and Laura Beth danced together on the floor.

Dad and Mom were sitting next to each other, holding hands, smiling and watching the festivities. Several times Dad said, "My, what an attractive family!" I wasn't sure he remembered what part he had played in this little family, but his expression showed he liked what he saw at that moment.

It was a beautiful, loving way to share our family connection.

Earlier in the day, as I started my car to head over to Bruce's house with the grandchildren, the radio blared out a song about old ladies and babies — Neil Diamond's, "Brother Love's Traveling Salvation Show." A song for our journey.

And I wasn't in charge.

Jake and Laura Beth

When Jake and Laura Beth's mother went on a cruise for a week, the kids stayed with Bruce. He normally kept them on Sunday and Wednesday nights and is usually a very available dad, but the day-in and day-out responsibilities can be draining for the custodial parent, based on my own experience during Carlton's first seven years of life.

Sunday night of that week, I was at Bruce's house eating supper with his family and looking at their schedule of after-school activities. Jake did karate and Laura Beth took dance lessons, and between the two of them every afternoon involved transportation. It reminded me of the hours I spent carpooling Carlton to *tae kwan do*, or boychoir, or baseball practice, and it looked like something Aunt Laura knew how to do, so I volunteered. The dinner conversation then shifted to a discussion about the best way to pick up the kids at after-school day care with the proper outfits for each scheduled activity.

When we finished eating, we put their gym bags in the trunk of my car, gave each other final instructions, and the week was ready for takeoff. Bruce seemed pleased, but hesitantly asked if I could also help with homework. OK, I knew how to do this, too, and agreed to be the homework hotline when they were really stuck, but a third and fifth grader as smart as these children shouldn't need much help.

The week went smoothly enough. I picked up one or both from day care and drove them to their lessons, where I waited for them to change into karate or dance clothes and bring me their bags now containing school uniforms. These two cherubs were notorious for leaving a trail of belongings wherever they went, so I tried to round up everything I could at this point to avoid circling back later. When I picked them up from the lesson to return them to their dad's, they changed their clothes again, repacked their bags for the next day's activities, and put them back in the trunk.

Throughout the week the homework hotline was not called, although I grilled each child about what work they had and whether or not they needed help every time they climbed into my car.

After their lessons on Thursday I took them to Bruce's house and stayed with them until midnight, while his band played a gig. My job was to serve them the chicken and dumplings Mother had made, supervise homework and baths, and get them into bed at a reasonable hour.

Things went amazingly well as we fell into a routine. After dinner there was an initial balk from Jake about the bath, reminding me of my own son at this age. With Carlton I spent much time trying to explain the virtue of cleanliness. This time, however, I just turned on the tub's faucet, left the bathroom, and began clearing the dining room table. There was no discussion. Jake climbed in and stayed a good thirty minutes.

Laura Beth used Jake's bath time to get full attention for herself. We sat together on the living room sofa and looked through the packages of pictures her dad had taken. She filled an empty photo album with the "best" ones, most of which included herself, then left it on her dad's bed as a surprise. Meanwhile Jake had emerged from the tub, put on his pajamas and planted himself in front of the computer. I wondered how many evenings Carlton got the attention, like Laura Beth, to do something of his choosing with me. Or, like Jake, to be left alone to make his own decisions. It seemed so obvious now.

Winding down from their busy lives, they were ready for bed by 8:30 without any fuss.

I finished cleaning the kitchen, replayed the evening in my head as if talking to my notebook, and reminded myself how complex this mother job is. And how important. It was so hard to know these things when I was in the middle of them.

This modern world gets busier and busier, and we drag our children along at its harried pace. We may be forgetting to schedule some unplanned time, just to be available.

Being available for myself is something I am learning better now, as I take constant notes on everything around me. Maybe we could all use some unscheduled time in our overwhelming lives to learn what else we want for ourselves and our children.

Appreciating Teachers

Teacher Appreciation Week means different things at different schools. When I worked at a middle-class magnet school, like the kind Carlton attended, I was inundated with homemade treats and teacher gifts. The PTA furnished lunch every day in the lounge, with specialties from the kitchens of parents or catered fare from local restaurants. We were all lavished with much more attention than any of us needed.

However, most of my teaching career had been in lower socio-economic schools, where parents spent most of their resources on survival, so gifts there were of a different kind. A spring picture hastily drawn on notebook paper and thrust at me by the young artist as she jumped off the bus. A cherubic face lighting up when he pulled out the four-inch carrot from our garden, or a reconnection with a former student now working at Wal-Mart, who enthusiastically recalled making dried worm candy as a second grader in my class.

These are precious, lasting gifts for sure, but there are times (like after a week of mandatory standardized testing) when teachers could use a little more obvious appreciation. My recently-retired teacher friend Kathy decided to do something special for our Stoner Hill friends on this designated week and called me Monday morning to solicit help, since we both had more time. Her idea was to provide lunch for them, and in our grandiosity we decided to offer more than sandwich trays and chips.

"What about the homemade comfort food of chicken spaghetti?" she proposed.

"Great," I quickly responded and volunteered to call the school secretary to find out which day would be best while Kathy perused her collection of cookbooks.

"Tuesday," Ms. Allred told me on the phone five minutes later, as she checked the school calendar.

"Tomorrow?" I asked.

"Yeah, that would be nice."

"OK," I replied, realizing we would need to get right to work.

Meanwhile Kathy had found a recipe that fed thirty. We could each make a complete recipe in our individual kitchens that afternoon to serve together in the teachers' lounge the next day, so we drove to Sam's

Wholesale Club to buy supplies in large quantities. It all sounded very logical.

But after shopping at Sam's we needed to stop at the local grocery store for some of the ingredients (only two bunches of celery instead of the ten pound package available at Sam's), and it was nearly two o'clock by the time we returned to Kathy's house to divide the supplies. When I finally got home with my share of ingredients, I immediately began boiling three large chickens in my two biggest pots and reading the recipe's fine print for the first time. It said to put the chicken stock in the refrigerator overnight to remove the fat. Hmm. As limited as my cooking confidence is, I had chosen not to veer from the printed instructions. That meant I would need to get up really early Tuesday morning to put the sauce together and let it simmer for four hours. So I chopped onions and celery, and de-boned chickens, getting all the ingredients ready for early morning bubbling. Halfway through this preparation I had to stop to run a cycle of dirty dishes. I needed a break from all the frantic kitchen activity. I walked into the living room, fell on the sofa, and picked up my pen.

This is getting complicated. I'm not sure I can do it. My kitchen isn't used to all this commotion.

Why did you want to do it in the first place?

Well, this school means so much to me. And these are my friends. I want to do something special. It's something I would have appreciated.

Then get off the sofa and back into the kitchen. That's how it'll get done.

The next morning I packed my car with freshly simmered homemade chicken spaghetti and headed to the little school on the hill. By 10:30 Kathy and I had set up a comforting luncheon in the teachers' lounge. Two hours later, after everyone had eaten, we put the leftovers in the refrigerator and repacked our cars with dirty pots and pans.

I was exhausted as I unloaded equipment from the car when I got home and moved on to the bedroom to collapse on the bed for a midday nap. But it was that satisfying feeling that comes from having successfully followed through on a plan.

However, a sandwich tray and chips might be our choice in the future.

Passing Notes

Before we left the lounge that day one teacher brought us a handwritten thank-you note on a Dr. Seuss card. It was cute and much appreciated, but not necessary. Watching the teachers enjoy the meal was all the thanks I thought I needed.

I realize I have mixed feelings about thank-you notes. Maybe it happened when as a child I was made to write them for Christmas gifts I didn't particularly want, or as a Southern bride when it became an endless task. It seemed a trade-off for all the attention I was receiving. I'm quite sure I passed those feelings on to Carlton, expecting him to communicate in a prescribed way.

Recently I got a thank-you note from a bride-to-be after having spent an hour of delightful conversation with her over a meal. She didn't need to send me a note; I thoroughly enjoyed the personal interaction.

And then there are all the baby showers I have attended, where guests sit around playing with the gifts and reminiscing about what our babies got and learning what's new on the market.

"Don't send me a note," I told an expectant mother, as I left her party. "It was enough to share your excitement."

She sent one anyway.

Thank-you notes aren't a bad thing. But neither is giving for the sheer joy of it, or seeing a gift or kindness once received passed on to someone else. So as my overactive mind began playing with this idea of notes, I thought of other kinds of written communications I felt confused about. Several times a week correspondence pops up on my computer in the form of e-mail chain letters. Some are clever little greetings or inspirational stories containing well-meaning wishes, but I'm asked to immediately send them to 15 of my closest friends, so these wishes will come true. I balk. It sounds pretty conditional.

My friend Robin forwards a lot of e-mail messages and some are chain letters. I told her I usually don't continue the chain, although I probably did at one time without thinking about it, going into my address book, hitting the forward button and moving on.

"That's OK," she chirped, "Just know that when I send you e-mail, it means I love you."

Oh, what a lovely thought. It still runs through my mind almost every time her name appears, and I tell others of her comment. Perhaps it is my way of forwarding Robin's message.

I received an inspirational story to pass on about someone at the grocery store giving a woman $50 to buy groceries. Sweet, I thought, and went about my morning routine, but a foundation had been set for the rest of the day. I realized later that in paying bills as part of morning business, I sent a $50 check to the local food bank. The request had been sitting in a stack on my kitchen counter for several days, but it wasn't until then that I finally acted on it. I was forwarding the e-mail.

After Carlton's death I received many cards and notes, some from people I knew long ago. I was amazed at the number and variety of people who responded, and I put the messages in a special box to reread periodically. Now when someone I know experiences the death of a loved one, I send a card, which is something I had never done before. It is another way of passing on the notes I have received.

Each of us wants to share love the best way we know how, the way it was shared with us, until we learn new ways. I want to be more deliberate about communicating love now. I want to think and say and do things to give meaning to these abstract feelings.

Two days after Kathy and I served lunch to our former colleagues a thank-you note came in the mail from Stoner Hill. It was a computer-generated design, signed by every staff member at the school. I smiled, reading through the three columns of names and knowing how much effort it must have taken to get all those signatures. Then I called Ms. Allred once again to express my appreciation.

A Writing Day

I usually begin my day writing several pages in my journal. Julia Cameron in *The Artist's Way* calls them morning pages. I jot down remembered dream pieces, review previous activities and thoughts, and plan for the upcoming day.

The obvious things are listed — a dentist appointment, a video that needs returning, a trip to the grocery store if there is no coffee, or Sunday afternoons with my writing friends. Then I follow it with some possibilities I might try.

So one morning began....

There is nothing on the calendar and the day is cold and overcast. Yesterday was a good writing day. Tomorrow I'll be teaching math to nurses for four hours. I want to make today another writing day.

After writing my journal entry I usually go to the computer to read the local paper's headlines and check my horoscope and e-mail. My brother Bruce had sent me a note casually asking about Jake, among other things. Gifted, creative, and sensitive, my nephew reminds me a lot of Carlton. His well-being is never far from my mind. I was not sure what to offer Bruce, but glad to be asked, so I postponed a reply until later, when I had a clearer idea.

My trusted yardman, once the custodian at the middle school where I taught, called. He was available for a pre-spring visit, and my yard certainly needed it. He has taken such good care of my lawn. I didn't want to turn him down, even though I had considered writing at the library this morning.

So I stayed on the sofa writing in my journal, as Mr. McMiller ran the mower outside. I should have been planning a math lesson for the nurses' review class I had agreed to teach. But rather than getting out the textbook, I got up to load the dishwasher and returned to the computer to reread Bruce's questions. I tapped out a tentative reply, editing and re-editing, and carefully clarifying my input as just opinion, before I offered observations. Help, God, I begged. Let my words be heard in love. This precious ten-year-old, who is funny, creative, and smart, was being told by the world to get serious. He's so much like his dad, and me, and Carlton. Maybe he's like a lot of people. This balancing act is hard. I reread my reply, took a deep breath, and hit the send button to launch my words into cyberspace.

I was now ready to tackle the math lesson. Assuming preparation for a four-hour class would take a while, I was pleasantly surprised when I opened the text to review what I taught the previous semester, and it all came back. I remembered what we spent time on, and how I broke up the long morning session with a variety of activities.

I would begin with a pretest and finish with a review of the lesson's experiences. The rest of the plan was a collection of activities to address possible deficits we discovered along the way.

I went to the education supply store for a new pack of flash cards in case we needed to review multiplication facts. While I was out, I stopped at the grocery store for milk and dog food, and impulsively tossed a couple bags of candy into my cart as incentives for the nursing students. The day designated for writing was rapidly filling up, and I had written no stories. I was a bit concerned, but still didn't write.

When I returned home the mail had come. Tucked among the advertisements and bills was a postcard Mother had sent. They are her form of e-mail, calling them her "postcards from the edge." This card was commenting on stories I had left at her kitchen door earlier — sections of my book. She had penciled positive, affirming statements; there were no suggestions or concerns. Was she learning to communicate differently? Was I learning to hear her differently?

Encouraged by her words, I went back to the sofa, picked up the loose-leaf notebook holding the stories I had written so far, and began to edit as I read through them. I saw common strands coming together. After an hour of work and feeling energized by the process, I drove to George's Grill for an early supper.

George's was not as noisy at that time of day. No clattering dishes sliding into a plastic tub or busy chatter of people connecting around the room, or constant ding from the counter bell signaling a ready order. A hamburger with smothered onions and extra crispy fries, was set before me and in the quieter setting I mentally journaled a review of my day. I had to let go of my plans to spend the day writing, but the day that unfolded had been a good one, spent as a loving sister and aunt, a competent teacher, and a mature daughter.

I returned home to settle on the sofa. I reached over to turn on the table lamp next to my storyteller doll, as it was dusk before I picked up my yellow tablet and pen to begin writing this story. It was the kind of day I had wanted after all, I scribbled, as I recalled all the activities I had participated in that invited clear and honest communication.

Nursing School

In the fall of 2003, I was asked to finish teaching a study skills class for LPNs because my friend Linda, who had been the instructor, was called to California to help her sick brother and his family. I was not sure exactly what I was agreeing to, but I could use a little extra money from a job description sounding much like the tutoring I did with Avery. So I improvised through the three remaining classes as best I could. Coming in after the semester began gave me little time to assess needs, much less provide for them, and I wondered what to offer twenty student nurses with a variety of academic abilities and experiences.

The next fall I was asked back to teach the study skills class, followed by a math review in the spring. The second course would try to remedy phobias and gaps in learning before the students took Dosage Calculation, a course which needed accurate math skills. I agreed, beginning the semester with the class, and having a clearer idea of what was expected from me and the students. The program, a satellite of Our Lady of the Lake College in Baton Rouge, was designed to address the local nursing shortage and provide a nurturing opportunity for those who wanted post-secondary career training.

I was quite aware of my own insecurities with math and didn't take the assignment lightly. I had to plan several four-hour review classes for seventeen students who had been vocal about their apprehension. I knew it wouldn't take much to add to those fears. I tried to be reassuring. "We really already know most of what we need. This is just a review." But despite my soothing words, several students flinched when I passed out the pretest.

"It's OK, y'all," I said, trying to find calming words again. "This isn't for a grade. It's just to see where we need to spend our time."

I checked their "tests" during the first break and noted emerging patterns. There were mistakes from carelessness in long division, not remembering how to reduce fractions to the lowest terms, or putting a decimal point in the wrong place. And for a couple of students there was a complete lack of knowledge of Roman numerals. But I found nothing that couldn't be systematically addressed.

I gave the pretests back as they were settling in for the next hour of class, and several began offering excuses. "It's OK, y'all," I repeated. "This isn't for a grade. It's just to see where we need to spend time."

For the first twenty minutes we reviewed Roman numerals. It went well, as most students felt confident with this information. One still seemed confused, but was willing to hold her questions until the next break.

My plan was to move on to multiplying fractions, so I wrote a problem on the board and immediately felt tension in the room. OK, fractions still stirred a little fear in me, too. I erased the board. We could begin with multiplication facts instead. I pulled out the newly purchased box of flash cards, and we proceeded to play "travel" around the room. One student stood next to her neighbor and I held up a multiplication problem. The person who correctly answered it first moved on to the next neighbor. It was a good review and icebreaker, as everyone had an equal chance to experience screw-ups and successes in front of the class.

After reviewing multiplication facts and building more confidence, I returned to the board and again wrote a multiplication problem with fractions. There was no obvious reaction this time, so together we worked through the equation. There were a couple more group problems, and then the students worked their own from the book, while I took notes in my journal about how this lesson was going. After we finished, volunteers came to the board to share their answers, and the rest of the class checked their work at their seats. Candy was offered to the volunteers. I was back in fifth-grade teacher mode and no one appeared too stressed.

Four hours later, there had been no mutiny. One student found her problem in regrouping, a simple subtraction deficit, while doing division. Another benefited by working step-by-step with a partner for the first six problems. Those who expressed concern at the beginning of class were now eager to tell me how much better they felt at the end.

What we discovered were little gaps in math knowledge, somewhere from the third or fourth grade, which had evolved into full-blown phobias as adults. In four hours with a little trip back in time, many of these tiny holes were being plugged.

This "teacher" story is about me, a reminder of my own fears and how I have been addressing them. Little gaps in knowledge that have developed into full-blown adult terror. I proceed baby-step-by-baby-step, changing activities, pairing with partners, trying games and group work, and even using candy as an incentive, while I tackle my own shadows. It's the teacher in me taking charge of my own learning.

At the Library

Early one morning after I had enjoyed several productive hours writing at home on my sofa, Princess wanted a walk. So I put on my tennis shoes and followed her suggestion.

After spending thirty minutes in the fresh air and sunshine the house felt too empty and dark and quiet. My inside voice was still talking to me, but it said, "Go write in public. You know how to do this around people."

I grabbed my woven bag and drove to the nearby branch library to sit in my safe place, a sunny window in the periodicals section overlooking the duck pond. Soon the amazing conversation running through my head was showing up on the notebook page, but I was in public. I didn't want to be a recluse, at least not full time. I've been scribbling and assimilating information for myself, and now I wanted to share it. I was not so special that I needed to be kept under glass like a hothouse flower, just because I journaled.

I had fifty years of being in the world before I started this intense inner journey, and looking back now, those years were certainly not a waste of time. They were the experiences on which my voice is based.

I looked up from my notebook and saw high school girls in uniforms. Could we connect, I wondered? I liked the relationship I shared with my outgoing niece and the self-sufficient Girl Scouts from the cruise.

A solitary young man was looking through the video section. Surely I could talk with him, having seen so many movies recommended by another solitary young man.

There were a couple of older women with stacks of books at the check-out counter. In addition to the fact they obviously enjoyed reading, I might also find common ground with them from what I have learned by getting to know my mother better.

Sometimes I fear I have gone so deeply into my own experience that I am too weird for the general public. The library outing was a good balance to a morning of monk-like quietness.

Just the other day I had successfully taught math to student nurses for four hours. That experience threw me back into the teaching world, where I once knew how to participate. But I confess to having a major panic attack trying to leave the house to teach the class. Having no time to journal, I called my friend Linda, once the principal at the middle school where I taught for nine years. She knew me as a teacher and the connection with her immediately calmed me down.

What is my fear? Am I really who I think I am? Is it because I really like the more-examined me, and I'm afraid the world could take her away? But then that's my choice, isn't it? The more-examined me knows when to retreat when she's running low on energy. But being out on a sunny day is a really healthy thing to do.

I'm still looking for safe places, as I gingerly stick my toes back into the stream of life. It's like that first cold rush in the early summer swimming pool as I let the water ease up to my knees, my waist, and my shoulders, feeling every stage intensely. Sometimes I wish I could just jump in all at once and get it over with.

A safe place is growing inside me as I learn how to take care of myself. That no matter what might happen, I can find the resources to survive, maybe even thrive wherever I am.

Math Anxiety

It was time to teach the algebraic formula called "dimensional analysis" that nurses use to convert medicine dosage, and I needed to review the process again for myself. For two weeks we had reviewed math concepts and measurement leading up to this skill. But my own math fear lurked just below the surface. If I showed any anxiety I might set off every other math-related phobia in the room. The ease Carlton displayed as he breezed through calculus and trigonometry obviously didn't come from me.

The day before class I worked each problem from the chapter in the safety of my living room, then checked it with the answers in the back of the book, step by step, articulating the process aloud. Princess moved away from her place in my lap to a more interesting section of the sofa. Apparently she had no desire to confront her own math limitations at this time.

Slowly and successfully I worked problems one through seven, remembering the tension I felt last semester working them on the board in front of twenty pairs of eyes. This time my plan was to over-learn each one and be as confident as possible.

On number eight I again named each step as I wrote the problem — identify the given quantity, identify the wanted quantity, and find the path by checking the conversion chart in the book for approximate equivalents. This was getting easier, I mused, quickly jotting down my answer and turning to the back of the book. Arrgh! It was a totally different answer. And, as if that was not enough, my eyes moved down to number nine's answer. It looked like the one I had for number eight. Arrgh, again. Maybe it was a mistake. Maybe the publisher switched the two. I looked back at both problems. It was not a misprint, and I had no idea where the answers came from. It made no sense to me.

I looked at my work again, then checked the conversion charts. My mind started spinning. Where did I go wrong when I thought I was being so careful? Of course that only added a new layer of anxiety to an already shaky situation.

But I immediately recognized that circling question; I had it often. "Where did I go wrong?" Arrgh. It was time to close the book and pick up my pen.

I'm taking a break from math anxiety and conversion charts and dimensional analysis until

I feel calmer. I need to change the subject and find some balance again. Then maybe I'll be able to start my little step-by-step process with number eight again. I'm being reminded of my own apprehension and how I get through it. Part of the preparation for tomorrow's lesson, I guess.

New Life

The End of Winter

One morning in March 2005, I woke with unclear ideas swirling in my head, building anxiety. At that time my mornings were usually calmer or full of new ideas; the unclear anxiety didn't come until later in the day. I picked up my pen and journal to sort out what it might mean.

So what's going on? Why am I feeling so anxious? How can I bring these fuzzy thoughts into focus? I'm beginning to feel out of control again.

This afternoon my friend Kathy and I are going to Jefferson, Texas, to a Pulpwood Queens Book Club meeting. The author of this month's selection will be there. We'll get there in time for the 6:30 meeting, then spend the night at the old Hotel Jefferson down the street. I need to get ready.

I put down my pen and tended to the chores I needed to finish before leaving town. A load of wash, a call to the vet, a couple of bills paid, and an e-mail to my brother with the hotel's phone number.

But when it was time to pack, I just stood in front of the crowded bedroom closet unsure of what to take. I couldn't find anything. I pulled out five sweatshirts and grabbed several long-sleeved turtleneck pullovers, then took this armload of warmer clothes to the hall closet. The weather was still cool in the morning, but this closet was so full I was getting overwhelmed just trying to decide what to wear.

Next I went to the sunroom to move the load of freshly washed laundry to the dryer and noticed the potted plants that have lived in this room all winter. They looked as if they might benefit from being back outside. It was almost Palm Sunday, the farmer's gauge for our last "cold snap," and these poor plants needed a resurrection. The sunroom is not very bright, and I hadn't been very faithful about watering them. Eight magenta bromeliad blossoms had unfolded in the last two months, as if trying to get my attention. So I dragged these scrawny house plants outdoors to the small, concrete patio just beyond the sunroom door for some healthy nurturing from Mother Nature.

Brushing the dirt and cobwebs from my hands, I officially declared an end to winter. A thorough spring cleaning could be in order, I mused, but quickly dismissed that idea. That's never been part of the season's greeting for me, and I was not that interested in beginning a new tradition now. There was no use getting carried away. I did, however, sweep around the area where the pots had been, cleaning up spilled dirt and dead leaves.

Then I drove to a nearby department store to buy a pair of basic black pants for the trip. It should have been an easy ten-minute errand because I would look for the same pair of pants in black that I bought in khaki last month. There was just one small problem. It's almost impossible for me to run into this store, purchase one item, and slip out. Something else always catches my eye as I wind my way through the maze of women's separates. This day was no exception. Within minutes I found myself in a dressing room trying on a brightly colored plaid shirt and a blue one with sequins. Sequins! I am not a bright-color, sequin-type dresser. What was this? I looked at my vibrant reflection in the mirror and felt like a flower. I bought both shirts, along with the basic black pants.

Driving home in my pollen-covered car, my spirit was stirred by the neighborhood azalea and dogwood blossoms and the brisk, clean air. Who could possibly resist participating in such an inviting renewal?

My focus was clearer. The swirling ideas in my head from the morning were just preparing me to take my place in the energizing environment of spring.

Looking for Spring

The calendar said spring would begin in two days, but the bright blue skies and budding trees didn't seem to be waiting. It had been two years and two months since Carlton's death and my mission on this day was to take Leah's kindergarten class on a hike around the schoolyard to find spring. We discovered tiny purple flowers on the redbud trees, clumps of yellow daffodils, flitting butterflies, crawling ladybugs, and fragrant wild onion flowers. It was hard to contain these puppy-like five-year-olds in such a playful setting. The surge of spring energy was obviously running through them, too. When we finally got quiet enough to listen for the sounds of spring, we heard a cacophony of birds, squawking much like I did, trying to rein in the children.

Back at home a male and female mallard duck sat in a neighbor's sweet gum tree, but before I had a chance to go outside and point them toward the nearby duck pond, they were off. How could anything stay centered on a day like this? Soon we would celebrate Easter and resurrection and here it was, in all its glory, demanding my attention. The stirring from winter's tomb — emerging sweet smelling flowers, sunny skies, dancing butterflies, lucky ladybugs, frisky children, singing birds, and returning ducks. Reassurance that life goes on. A few days later I sat with my journal.

How can I hold onto the amazing warmth and light I feel in my heart? The stirring of joy in my soul? How can I remind myself that this happens year after year? That each turn of the seasons was important to spring's new growth? Last years' flowers become fruit in the heat of the summer, dropping their seeds to the ground in autumn to remain through the long winter months, as the Earth subtly shifts its position on its circle around the sun.

Today is the official vernal equinox, yet the other 364 days of the year had been preparing for its arrival.

When I pulled weeds from my garden, I felt the sun on my back and the stretch in my winter-atrophied muscles. I was a butterfly, slowly emerging from my cocoon, spreading my new wings, and allowing them time to strengthen and dry in the sun.

I want to remember these special moments — the way they look and sound and smell and feel. I want to be able to recall them on days when my heart needs a bit more warmth or my soul needs a little more joy. For 55 years I've experienced this cycle — this pheno-menon arriving as spring, and today I do so with all the awareness I can muster, like it's the first time, and with a determination that it will not be the last. I want to be able to pull it forth and replay it any day of the year, over and over again.

Writing as Spiritual Practice

The news was not good. The war in Iraq, rising gas prices, violent crimes, terrorism threats, and endless lawsuits filled the television screen. Anxiety built inside me as I watched these images. How would I survive with all this negative activity? What could I offer as a creative response for a hurting world? These were the issues Carlton and I discussed the last time we talked. We shared our frustrations. He said it was time for a people's awakening.

One thing I knew to do was go to my Sunday afternoon writing group. They weekly affirmed my writing and encouraged me to explore what was coming from my pen. But on this day everyone sounded so angry; their writings were the same rants and judgments I had heard on television. When it was my turn to read, I began by apologizing for my naive little-girl writing, and I didn't like that about myself. When the group didn't break up at its regular time, continuing instead to feed on its angry words, I knew I had to leave. I drove home with an unsettled feeling. I needed to talk to my notebook.

Why can't I just let them be that way? Why did it make me so anxious? These are writers. We share a common bond. But I've been writing to find peace, serenity, and a feeling of redemption. I'm eager to share

what it is I am finding, and I'm tired of the
television news confronting me with its
endless problems. I need energy to confront
my own. I know this world is a mess and I'd
like to offer hope, but I'm not always sure
how. The only thing I feel sure of at the
moment is that I don't want to add to the
negative discussion. When I feel frustrated
with the news, I shut it off, and when I'm
in a group of people spinning on this negative
energy, I say what I can, then leave. If I get
home and my insides are still churning, I
write. I don't know any other way for now.
I believe I have been filling these journals in
search of my own peace of mind. I don't
want to add to the suffering of others.
Today I shared the piece "Looking for
Spring," my simple way to consciously take
in the visible rebirth all around me, and I
apologized for it. Apologized for it! Why, for
goodness sakes? Maybe the fight I am having
is with myself. Maybe I wonder why I
continue to question my work. I want to
share my serenity with this talented group of
people. I want to be able to stay in this
messy world and find light and hope. Maybe I
believe these writers have similar potential,
but just need to be reminded. Maybe I need
to remember that I too am a talented writer
with potential. Ah, there's the affirmation I
wanted. The encouragement I needed to
explore what is coming from my pen. The
reminder of how I find creative responses
for my own hurts. Maybe it's my middle-age
hippie contribution to a people's awakening.

Making Friends with the Critic

As I wrote and edited the stories for this collection I was constantly confronted with a very vocal and determined voice inside my head. For days or weeks she could keep me away from writing anything except journal observations for my eyes only. When I picked up the legal pad I have set aside for developing stories I want to share, she began filling my head with nagging doubts.

"You don't know really what you're talking about, do you?" she brayed. "What do you think you're doing? Why would anyone want to read this?"

I quickly set the tablet down, picked up the friendlier marbled composition book and began jotting notes to myself again.

Little Ms. Perfect, where did you come from? Was it because I was once a language arts teacher and every red mark I ever scratched on a child's paper, pointing out the all important incomplete sentences or misplaced modifiers, has come back to haunt me? I was a teacher, not a writer, as I passed judgment on others searching for their voices.

Is it because my beautiful, talented child killed himself? It must have been something dreadful that I did. I was, after all, his mother. Who are you, screaming in my head with so many critical thoughts and shaming words? How do I convince you I am doing the best I can?

Fortunately, when the overwhelming news of Carlton's death arrived, I had been listening to another voice, the quieter one that gently penned loving words into my composition book, helping me sift through all the noise.

But now with an intense desire to share my story and a belief that if I told it in an honest way it could have meaning for others, all I could do was sit paralyzed on the sofa and stare at the yellow pad. Was I still afraid of the voice of the language arts teacher, haunting me with technical difficulties? Or the mother whose only child committed suicide?

Of course, the rather large stack of past rejection letters in my guest room did not add to my confidence. Their presence continued to remind me that anything I have ever written is nothing anyone else would ever want to read. At least that's what the fussy critic told me.

I wanted to be able to write more than daily ramblings to myself. I'd been removed from the world long enough. I believed these fears and doubts I've been listening to in my grief were universal, and if I could risk sharing my journey with others we could connect. How do I work through her noisy self?

One thing my notebook has taught me is that I cannot be a better speaker without becoming a better listener. Maybe all I needed to do was compassionately pay attention. Listen to what she was telling me of her experiences. Let her teach me how to speak to her.

So, Little Ms. Critic, never any farther away than my overactive imagination and lingering past regrets, you can hang around if you want. You are the voice that keeps me honest and alert. But I think it's only fair to let you know, you are not the only one I listen to now. My gentle pen isn't completely convinced of all your anxious concerns. It seems I still have a story I want to share.

The Creative Urge

I'm having another day of avoiding the yellow pad, wondering if I'll ever be a writer. All I can do is scribble in my notebook and watch my thoughts appear on paper. Ah, so here I am in black ink on white paper, showing myself how creative I can be. I can write myself back into existence.

Christmas, 2003, nearly a year after Carlton's death, I sent handmade cards to special friends who had been so supportive on my journey, congratulating them on being entered into the National Angel Registry. Two of my friends asked me how to get in touch with the registry so they could nominate others, and I had to sheepishly admit to making the whole thing up. Maybe I was warning them of my awakening imagination.

In 2004 my pen began spitting out short thoughts, proverbs, little sayings. It didn't seem to take as much effort as a story, but it was satisfying when I couldn't find courage to commit to anything bigger. I filled small notebooks with these brief efforts, shared them at my writing group, and received encouragement. I was connecting. I might be dancing around a bigger idea, but at least I was moving in the right direction. Maybe it was a warm up-exercise.

When visiting Oregon with my mom I took pictures of a hand puppet from Leah's class enjoying the sights, then made a book for the kindergarteners. The positive results motivated me to rewrite the story for my family and make everyone a spiral bound copy for Christmas. I now had a "published book." It felt as if I had cleared some kind of a hurdle.

My creative energy continued to look for ways to connect.

I made bracelets with clear beads and elastic string for the five-year-olds to wear to remind them they are children of God, then wore one on my wrist to remind my own kindergarten self. When the opportunity arose I took mine off and passed it on to a friend.

I brought home smooth, round, quarter-sized stones collected from the beach in Oregon and gave them to the kindergarten and nursing students. "Don't Worry Stones" I called them because Mother Nature's salt tears have already worn them smooth. I knew this from the personal experience She and I shared in October at the seashore.

Christmas 2004, I again felt the creative call, so I handed out magic mirrors, face down, to friends and family. I told the recipients that if they wanted to see a child of God, all they had to do was turn theirs over and look in. I kept one for myself.

In 2005 I filled dozens of tiny plastic Easter eggs with fuzzy baby chicks from the craft store and added a message folded like a fortune cookie. It said, "Break out of your shell and sing." One egg still sits on my kitchen window now, a morning reminder as I pour my first cup of coffee.

I know these activities have been necessary for me, reminding me of my ability to create. But I believe they were also opportunities to teach me how to connect to others. So I continued to scribble in my notebook, filling myself with new ideas. And when I felt full, I found ways to release my creativity.

It's how Mother Nature spreads seeds, and I smile at such a pleasant image.

The Pen as Witness

Every time I looked over this evolving collection of stories emerging from my constant journaling, I saw new patterns. Sentence by sentence, story by story, I was rebuilding myself. In the darkness and in the shattered illusion of who I thought I was, I had recorded each person, place, event, or idea that came to share their light with me, like the flickering votive candles in a Catholic church.

I didn't do this "coming back" into the world by myself. Most of the time during the first few months, and often thereafter, I didn't really want to stay here. I wanted to leave and find Carlton, whom I perceived as my scared child, and thus relieve myself of my own overwhelming fears. I would lie motionless on the sofa as something separated and lifted from my body. But all I could do was watch. I couldn't end it. There was unfinished business I wanted to address; it was not my time to leave. I kept picking up my pen and writing myself back into existence.

Look, Laura, you're still here and life is happening all around you.

I don't care. I don't like being here.

Well think about it. Write down your thoughts and don't take any other action just yet.

But, God, you don't understand. It's real painful down here. It's not fun.

I know, Laura. I know. Just hold on a little longer.

So I would hold on a little longer, making notes to myself about the pieces of this world I liked. Avery, Stoner Hill, my friends, and my dog were all diligently documented. And word by word these gentle loving pieces of light were woven together to create a brighter glow.

I even discovered that bleeding into my notebook was releasing pain and uncovering more light that my fear had been hiding.

I began finding other reasons to stay. People were telling me how well I was doing. I liked the affirmation and hesitated to tell them otherwise, so I kept writing, telling myself how well I was doing.

I liked the things my pen told me about myself and the world around me. They were tender, nurturing words, as if from a minister or counselor or teacher. Was this God? Was this the loving parent for the scared child?

My pen had been gently, patiently talking me back into the world, showing me light and beauty amidst all the pain, and teaching me how to recognize the unconditional love I hungered for.

I continue to write, the pen as my witness, reminding myself I can't leave now. There is too much unfinished business. There are other scared "children" who need this amazing love I continue to find, and now it's my turn to share with them — the way Avery, Stoner Hill, Princess, my friends, and my pen have done with me.

Make Me Feel Better

Several years before Carlton died, a long-time best friend sent me a letter telling me I was too needy, then put a moratorium on our friendship. It hurt, as I read it over and over, trying to understand. I wasn't available when she needed me, and this was her response. She wouldn't be available to me. But because she had been such a close friend for so long, I also took that comment very seriously, agonizing over what I did that appeared to be so needy to others.

What's causing this behavior? Is it my ego taking valuable resources from others? I don't mean to take more than my share. Maybe I am letting others take too much from me. Like the food chain. But I'm human, with free will and something more than instinct. How do I get myself into such a feeding frenzy?

I struggle with my part in the world's problems as I watch the evening news, and am convinced I have much to account for. But maybe I also just like the attention that comes from playing the martyr. How can I expect anyone else to participate in an honest conversation with me, when I'm having so much trouble being honest with myself?

I need to see these words before I hurl them out into the Universe. Let my neurotic lambaste the narcissist, and the narcissist return the favor. My own personal drama played out in the safety of my notebook. Me, the human animal juggling shame and blame, bad and good, shadow and light. Dr. Jekyll and Mr. Hyde.

Tell me I matter. Reassure me. Make me feel better. Please don't let me expect others to fix me, and begin that feeding frenzy all over again.

Don't let me impress them with my accomplishments. Or intimidate them with my anger or power. Or overwhelm them with my depression or my innocence. Back and forth, over and over, I can mindlessly manipulate words and actions trying to get the response I want.

Does this behavior make me a bad person? My self-will imposing itself on others. I don't mean it as bad. But its destructive quality is only amplified when I deny it or believe I'm somehow not like everyone else. My feelings are real to me. They are based on my experiences, my source to tell me who I am.

When I hurt, I write. When I get lonely, I converse with my pen. I feel fear and turn to the safety of my notebook. Make me feel better, I plead, and as if by magic, the swirling ink knows just what to say, how to comfort my pain, loneliness, and fear, using healing words stored deep within me. It's the still small voice that sings to me through a Uniball Gel Grip pen. Then after listening to this calming song of myself, I can go back out into the world with a confidence and kindness that comes from truly feeling better. With this awareness I can recognize my feelings for what they are and take them back to my notebook, if I need to, before I inflict them on someone who doesn't have the resources to help.

My dear friend who told me I was needy gave me a priceless gift, the kind only a true friend can give. A challenge to look at myself, and the time and space to do so. A wake-up call. The push I needed to learn how to take better care of myself, without being so dependent on others. A lesson on how to be my own best friend.

Releasing Shame

One night I received a phone invitation to a casual dinner party with people I wanted to reconnect with. The conversation was pleasant, but when I hung up, anxiety raced through my body. What still triggered that feeling? I finished one satisfying phone call with a good friend, but an hour later this one set off alarms.

I don't know what to bring. I'm not sure I'll fit in. I'm afraid I'll get lost following his directions to their new home in the country. They

invited me based on the me they knew
five years ago. I'm not sure who I
was then. I feel so much more
aware of myself now. What if I am
too different? What if they've
changed their minds about me? I
don't feel safe and I'm not sure
why. Why am I so scared? Why do
I think I should know more?

God answers Job by asking where
he was when the world was
created. Job's not supposed to
understand everything. That's
impossible. Let go and trust there
is a big picture. Tend to your own
little path. You'll learn what you
need to know when you need to
know it.

So every time I feel shame for messing up and not
knowing better, I guess this retired schoolmarm is
forgetting to let go and trust the process — the
process of learning. But it's been a long, painful journey
of letting go of the if-only-I-had-knowns and then
forgiving myself.

All I know to do now is pay attention to everything
that crosses my path and recognize the invitations to
participate in life again.

My son went west to seek his fame and fortune, and
I stayed here to find mine. As my journey takes me
deep into this experience of Carlton's death, I am
discovering a treasure I wasn't expecting. My life.

So what about the party? I had been invited; they must want me to come. That was all I knew for sure, and by knowing better who Laura is, perhaps I would bring exactly what I needed to bring. It would probably be a lot of fun. After all, I wanted to reconnect with them. Maybe they just wanted to do the same with me.

So the next day I got ready. I had decided what to bring. I got my offering and the written directions to their house and climbed in the car, backed out of the driveway, circled the block and pulled back into the garage. All I could do was sit in the car and cry. When I finally dragged myself into the house, I fell on the sofa and picked up my pen in resignation.

I can't do it. I'm a failure. No wait. That's not true. I've been learning what triggers my fears. And I have to recognize those triggers before I can do anything about them. I'm learning what I need to know.

In God's Hands

Those were words I said to Carlton in December 2002, the last time I talked to him. He had quit his job and was rather evasive about how he was looking for another one. I didn't know how to get any more out of him without sounding too pushy. He had assured me he was OK for money a couple months earlier, but none of us knew there was to be a slowdown in computer jobs and financial strife in the Golden State. At least I didn't know.

We had an interesting conversation about the state of the nation as it teetered on the brink of war, the paranoia stirred by 9/11, the Patriot Act, homeland security, and a growing need for a people's awakening. I heard his concerns. He was having a hard time watching the evening news, too. I heard him ask if I knew why I was here, and his statement that he wasn't sure why he was. I said he would figure it out, trying to reassure him; I wasn't sure when I was his age. I wish I had told him that *he* was what gave my life meaning when I was 27. But I was busy questioning my own reasons to be here at age 55, after retiring from teaching to write. I barely knew how to reassure myself. I heard his request for money and told him I was rather strapped. He said that's OK, or at least that was what I heard; I was concerned about my own ability to exist on a teacher's retirement. I listened as best I knew how, but I was distracted by my own doubting voice.

I told him I loved him and was putting him in God's hands. Again, it was what I was trying to do for myself. Maybe he didn't want statements like that. Maybe those were empty words for a scared child. What did they mean? What did he hear? Maybe he wanted something less abstract, something easier to understand. I was his mom; I should have known. But I wanted something less abstract myself, something easier for *me* to understand.

There have been so many times I wanted to rewind that conversation and start over. I believed he was finding himself, like he said he was, because I needed to believe I was finding myself. I believed he was OK where he was because I needed to believe that about me. They sound like such empty words now. What did he mean? What did I hear?

I asked if he wanted to come back to Shreveport and look for a job around here. He said no. When he didn't want to talk about the job search, I didn't pursue it. He'd been so eager to leave, and still pushed me away if I asked too many questions. Now I wish I had asked more. Maybe I could have done it gently. Maybe I should have risked being rejected again rather than fight the regret.

I knew he tried suicide once before, but I thought getting out of Shreveport was what he wanted, so I got out of his way and let him go, like a good mama bird. He just wasn't a very loud squawker, and there were more than enough noisemakers, both around me and in my head, vying for attention.

I didn't know what was going on with him then because I was busy trying to figure out what was going on with me. No wonder I didn't know how to help better. I was recovering from an unhealthy marriage that still had too many unanswered questions, and 30 challenging years of public school teaching. I had left organized religion after a lifetime of belonging, frustrated with the worldly side of it. I was trying to find balance in my new, all-consuming passion for writing. I had aging parents in town, one showing obvious signs of dementia and the other mirroring his behavior.

Help, God. I thought the decision I made to pull away and take care of myself was a healthy one.

Maybe Carlton's pulling away and taking care of himself was where I got the idea. Maybe he was checking to see if I could give him a reason to come back. So he called. And I, busy looking for my own reasons to stay, didn't know how to help. I don't like feeling that responsibility. I didn't like all the responsibility I felt in my marriage, in teaching, in working for my church, and in tending to my parents. But he was my son. He should have had first priority.

Where did I go wrong? Maybe I had let too many louder, fussier voices take over. I was just beginning to hear the sweet, quiet song of my pen, and it had given me the confidence to leave the church, retire, and tell my parents I couldn't move in with them.

But then I said to Carlton, "I don't know how to help."

I agonized after that phone call. What else did he need me to hear? How could I have gotten him to tell me more? What else did he want to hear from me? All I knew to do was keep writing in my journal, hoping answers would appear. They were, in my own handwriting, in my own voice. I just couldn't yet see or hear them. They were the words to teach me how to communicate better with others by learning how to communicate better with myself, and I had not learned how to turn such honest conversation outward.

I can still feel grief when that conversation runs through my head, wishing I knew then what I know now. I was doing the best I could, as I learned of myself. Today I have ways to watch and listen more selectively to myself and the world around me. The awareness of my participation in an unhealthy marriage has become clearer, and my parents don't look to me for their care.

Every face I see, including the one in the mirror, can be Carlton. The quiet ones especially get my attention; I guess those are the ones who have his voice. I don't always know how to help, and I still put all of us in God's hands. Those words are not empty to me. Maybe I just needed to learn how truly powerful they can be.

I don't like thinking of this as God's plan, that Carlton's earthly death was necessary for my own life to become more authentic. My beautiful son chose to leave, and it became my responsibility to choose to stay. Once upon a time his birth saved my life and now, it seems, facing his death is saving it again.

Life on Earth is a process. If I can't move on from this experience, I leave with him. So I write, day after day, page after page, asking myself more questions, listening to my answers, and then watching for opportunities to take my improved communication skills back into life.

Blessed Are the Empty

The beatitudes are such a paradox. They certainly didn't make much sense to me as a child. How in the world could the meek inherit the Earth? What would they do with it, for Pete's sake? Or the poor in spirit getting to be the ones to see God? Now that seemed highly unlikely to my way of thinking.

So I was given other ways to try and understand them. Substitute the word "happy" for "blessed," the Sunday school teacher would say. Well that didn't make much sense to me either. Happy are those that mourn? Yeah, right. That was not my experience.

Then there was the suggestion to break up the word beatitude. Be attitude. Make it a plan of action. Be meek, be poor in spirit. Be mourning. Hmmm. I did not like where that was going. This beatitude stuff was tricky.

As a young adult the one I liked best was, "Blessed are the peacemakers, for they shall be called the sons of God." (Matthew 5:9 NKJV) I add "and daughters" after sons. I was a passionate hippie protesting the violence of the Vietnam War with angry, accusing placards and loud, long marches. Didn't that qualify me as a peacemaker? How come all I seemed to stir up was an equal confrontational reaction? Where was my reward, I smugly wondered. I was screaming for peace to the outside world, not hearing it as a cry deep within myself.

Now I have my own beatitude. One for the less naive me, based on my experience of darkness as the paradox for finding light.

Blessed are the empty, for they shall be filled.

On January 11, 2003, the contents of my rather self-satisfied cup of happiness were spilled. Spilled? Shoot, the whole cup was shattered, for me and everyone else to see. Oh dear. Was this the end to any claim of innocence? Did I have to learn my lesson the hardest way possible? Was there another way out, or did I have to go straight through it?

When I first got the phone call, I was numb to all feeling, uncertain if I even still existed, or wanted to. Then as feelings returned, I trusted few conventional routines to tell me how to begin gathering up my shattered bits. I was scared of everything, except my pen and a few gentle friends. I had to learn a new way to rebuild, so I wrote. As I restructured myself with something lighter *and* more substantial, I could continue to clean out the layers of fears and regrets, as they were uncovered.

This has been my life review. Fifty years of how Laura has been defined. Reactions to the stimuli around me, as I learned to survive on earth. And now, releasing past responses I no longer want or need, I can make more deliberate, honest choices.

Emptying. To be fulfilled. It's a constant act of letting go and accepting the light from within and without. How could I have known more? I was doing the best I knew. I had to learn that I needed new ways.

Now I journal my thoughts, remove myself from situations that make me too anxious, consider what those feelings mean for me, and find ways to take care of myself, day by day. And each morning I wake to a list of intentions, aware that invariably throughout the day there will be adjustments. I am practicing the process of emptying from my egotistical expectations and desires, to be filled with a greater plan.

Blessed are the empty, for we shall be filled.

Letting Go

My loyal Dell laptop was driving me crazy. I bought this particular computer based on Carlton's recommendation.

"Get a Dell," he said, "because they have great tech support."

I didn't realize then that great tech support to him and great tech support to me meant two entirely different things. If I ran into a problem all I had to do was call an 800 number and this very patient guy could talk me through it. But the process was complicated because I didn't have enough computer knowledge to know what he was talking about, which raised my stress level and tried his patience. OK. I didn't really want to know how to troubleshoot my own computer, so I found a local repair service. Merlin Computers. I chose it for the name. I needed something magical to get me through this labyrinth.

The computer's capacity, more than adequate five years earlier, was now rather limiting, even after Mr. Merlin added more memory. I trudged on.

Then as I was loading a new ink cartridge, the printer went nuts and the cartridge got lodged inside the printer case. I couldn't get to it. Argh. I took it to Mr. Merlin, the magician. After performing a C-section to remove the breech cartridge, he told me some little piece (he may have actually named it) was broken and would probably cause a slow leak inside the printer. Oh, great. But then he made the mistake of telling me that it would probably keep working for a while, and that was the part I heard, so I plugged it back into my computer and returned to work.

There was, however, a problem that was getting the best of me. I used my computer mainly as a word processor and for e-mail, and after all these years, it had developed an irritating stutter. I would type a story at a passable speed, only to look up and see little red squiggly lines underlining every other word, telling me they were misspelled. Well, I didn't purposely type "seemed" with six e's. This was becoming too much work. I wanted to spend my energy writing stories, not typing them.

So I drove to Office Depot to look at their computers. I didn't really know what I wanted, except that I didn't need the tech support of Dell. I needed advice, and this time I couldn't depend on Carlton. A nice young man saw me reading descriptions of the displays and may have also been able to read the clueless look on my face. (And the word "gullible" tattooed on my forehead.)

"Well, I'm just looking," I said, afraid he would launch into a jargon that might as well be Japanese.

"Do you know what you want?" the nice young man asked.

"Not really. I know what I use my computer for, but I don't want that to limit future possibilities."

Then we went to a monitor to "build" a custom computer. He asked questions, I answered them, and he made recommendations. OK, I realized I was pretty vulnerable here, but this was not an area I wanted a lot of control over. We talked over options, then he gave me some choices and a preliminary price. Well, it wasn't cheap, but still in the ballpark (Yankee Stadium, maybe).

I couldn't make a decision and I told him this, so he printed out the "custom" computer's specs for me to go home and think about.

I left the store, tended to a couple errands, and found myself pulling into the bank, to transfer money from my savings account. I couldn't let go of this thing. I had no really good reason to put it off. As soon as I left the bank, I headed straight back to Office Depot with my printout in hand, put in my order, paid the cashier, and proudly walked out with the receipt.

Money was one of the issues holding me back while I insisted my old computer was good enough. When Carlton made and spent a lot of money in California, I worried. Obviously, having a Scottish father who grew up during The Depression made a big impression on me.

And the Dell laptop was a link to Carlton – the computer he picked out for me in 2000. That day I understood it was time to let it go.

Consider the Lilies

"Consider the lilies of the field, how they grow; they neither toil nor spin, yet I tell you, even Solomon in all his glory was not clothed like one of these." (Matthew 6:28b-29 NRSV)

Another story was coming together as Princess flopped like a puddle across my legs. *Relax,* she reminded me. It was the gift of her royal presence.

My needs were being met. Not necessarily the way I would have planned. But I had been given an interesting mix of people, places and events, and ideas to sustain me. I had wasted a lot of energy struggling when life didn't match my expectations. I was fighting the Universe and everyone else's plans.

The blessings I was sent weren't always my first or second choices, or any I thought I might have, but then my idea of choices had been based on limited past experiences. There was the teenaged angel Avery, a nurturing group of teacher and writer friends, a fantasy cruise vacation, and enough insurance money to release me from some of my financial worry. I had a quiet comfortable house, a sunny library nearby, and a magical little school that continued to welcome my desire to connect. There were also the new beginnings of weddings and spring, playmates of all kinds, and a curiosity and creativity constantly challenging my former knee-jerk need for control. And a pen that documented everything.

What will I do today, or tomorrow, or next week? All I have to do is look behind me, at where I've been. I recorded it for a reason. It is my proof that I have been given what I need when I need it. And time to understand and appreciate the "present" as a "gift."

As I wrote these words the washing machine in the next room pounded a rhythm for my dancing pen, and the "book" became clearer. By the end of April 2005, I took a final trip to the Rocky Mountains of Colorado to present a draft of my "complete" manuscript. That May, Avery graduated from high school with sights and plans set beyond her hometown. In June, I took another cruise with Patricia, but this time to the frontiers of Alaska, without teenagers. And my once-new computer, full of potential, continues to accept and store my ongoing thoughts.

In one week I was part of two different audiences, as real-life authors shared personal experiences sounding much like my own. The nursing students took their math final, and everyone made 96% or higher. And Laura Beth, my precocious third-grade niece, timidly showed me her "writings" — her own journal, recording interactions with her friends. My eyes teared up with joy.

Life is abundant, with more than enough to sustain me. But I had to learn this by letting go of expectations and attachment to my plans, accepting what is, and recognizing that I, like Job, can't possibly know all my choices.

I'm not ready for my journey on Earth to be finished, even though I'm sure it will be full of new challenges. I want to keep trusting that my life unfolds in a beauty and awe beyond anything I can imagine. With the help of my pen, I will continue to welcome the adventure.

Master Teacher

The study skills class for nursing students used a book entitled *Becoming a Master Student.*

What kind of teacher thinks she can teach students to be masters of their own learning? Wouldn't it need to be someone confident about her own ability as a student? One who could assess where she is, and what lessons she needs? One who is able to choose effective methods and materials to fulfill the lesson's objectives, then check for understanding and be ready to offer an alternative method if re-teaching is in order? One who knows how to affirm and guide herself, finding assurance that mistakes are opportunities to learn information that hasn't yet been mastered? Yikes! This sounds pretty self-actualizing.

I was not sure how I could fine-tune my first sixty stories and write two more to "finish" this manuscript before I went to the final meeting of my Colorado writing group. What I was looking for was a concise bottom line to wrap up this meandering journey, and I realized that was no small task. But I needed to put words on paper; there was no more time for experimenting. A conclusion was in order.

So the master teacher/student kicked into action and formulated an effective lesson plan, using a standard form from years of classroom practice.

Objective:

- The learner will write two more stories to complete the manuscript, *Writing Toward the Light: A Grief Journey.*
- The learner will continue editing previous stories to tighten the continuity of said manuscript.

Materials:

- Pen, yellow tablet, previously written stories, computer, blue-flowered sofa, journal, and watercolors.

Procedure:

- Journal — begin with warm-up journaling. Natalie Goldberg's timed writings or Julia Cameron's morning pages are effective exercises to clear out all other thoughts vying for the student's attention.
- Sit still. Breathe. Breathe again. Repeat as necessary throughout the lesson.
- Journal again to continue clearing out the distracting thoughts that are still getting in the way of the student's focus.
- If a creative release is still needed, and words are not yet obvious, paint a picture.
- (Recess) Take a walk in the park for exercise, fresh air, centering, and for reminding the student where she gains strength.

- Eat lunch. (Do not omit this step.)
- Drive to the library. Look through the movie titles or new book arrivals. These are finished products as motivation for what you are trying to accomplish. Take a sunny seat by the window.
- Settle in with pen and tablet and begin writing.

Evaluation:

- Lesson is successfully completed when the two exercises are written.

Did I finish? Not that day. This was only the plan that needed to be continually adjusted as I assessed how much preparation I needed and how to best meet that need. It got me through the first of two stories. Then I needed to rewrite parts as I typed the story into the computer and revisited it several times over the next few days. When I was somewhat satisfied with this story, I could begin the final one. The one to sum up my experience of searching for light with the help of a pen. Of course, after the final story was rewritten, there would be a zillion other adjustments throughout the book.

It was a beginning to an ending, which was probably just a new beginning. A master student knows her learning is never finished.

A Child's Spirit

Where is Carlton? What happened to the light that was my son? I am introduced to his loving spirit through every person, place, thing, or idea that comes my way (and some have had to come my way many times before I see they, too, are Carlton's light) — those named and unnamed in this collection of experiences. He is everywhere I use my eyes and ears to find love.

One Sunday he was at the Trapped Truth Society meeting with my writer friends, eager to share their voices. Later that evening he was with us at my brother's house, as Bruce grilled chicken for supper, and Avery, Jake, and Laura Beth reported their latest school news. On Monday morning he was at George's Grill eating a scrambled egg and bacon sandwich and solving the world's problems with me and my brother Buddy.

Tuesday he was sitting in the calm, clean dayroom at the Northeast Louisiana War Veterans Home in Monroe with my mom and dad, a dozen war vets, and several cheerful attendants.

During the day on Wednesday he stretched out with me and Princess on the sofa in the middle of my living room to watch a dancing pen edit another dozen stories. That night he tried a new restaurant with

Linda and me, as we shared the communion of our sacred friendship.

On Thursday at Stoner Hill he was with the kindergarteners painting watercolor blossoms for "Miller's Garden," and singing and dancing to the song, "Each of Us Is a Flower." That night he walked a labyrinth, spread out on the gym floor of Linda's church, with a dozen other silent sojourners and me.

Friday he lunched with the nurturing teaching staff from Our Lady of the Lake nursing program at Dena's sunny country home, and later that afternoon he connected at the circular table at Nicky's Mexican Restaurant with the Steel Magnolias.

He is here and there and everywhere in between — at the grocery store and the park, in the library, on the phone, through e-mail and snail mail. As loving connections are made from one energy source to another, Carlton's light flashes, or sings, or dances, or smiles, or scribbles, or cries. Everywhere I am, he is. I carry his spirit with me. The stirring, the warmth, the assurance I once felt in my womb and found again on the Caddo Lake Nature Trail, where his ashes are now spread, flows through my entire body.

And the void, that incredible darkness on the night of January 11, 2003, was just an illusion, my overwhelming fear hiding the light I had known. Carlton's spirit has been here all along, patiently waiting for me to learn how to see it, hear it, and reconnect with it.

I had my own near-death experience as I tried to follow my son. But there was no great white light for me to walk toward. On that first night I grabbed hold of the two things I could trust, Leah and my pen. Leah provided me with initial safety through connections outside myself, and the ink from my pen identified flickering lights within me and gathered them together to form the brighter light that is my life now. I carry this journey with me — a combination of little Laura and little Carlton and every daughter and son of God we come in contact with. And that is where I find my child's spirit.

Safety, reaching out, connections, renewed energy, and ultimately new life. It's all God, and it's always there, ready to replace the cold, dark illusion of fear with the warmth and assurance of love. It will always be there, for it is a force death can not extinguish, a force made stronger for me by my own death experience.

It is now my responsibility to continue seeing, hearing, and sharing this connection, this light, this love, this energy spirit I call God, wherever my path leads me.

An Attempted Ending

I approached Carlton's thirty-first birthday, still looking for a way to end this book, when it finally dawned on me. There is no ending. Nothing is really ever "finished." Everything becomes information and experience, a foundation for what is to be.

My focus, to be finished, was my frustration. It's a journey, the wise ones say. And mine is still being recorded in a journal. Daily, one step at a time, one word after another. The acceptance phase of the grief process. Not acceptance because we're "supposed" to be grateful, but with open arms, like the little guy on the previous page. Bring it on, God. Let me be immersed in life. Elisabeth Kübler-Ross said, "It's only when we truly know and understand that we have a limited time on Earth — and that we have no way of knowing when our time is up — we will then begin to live each day to the fullest, as if it was the only one we had."

And what have I learned from my journey thus far? Better ways to take care of myself and accept the gift of life. The ability to find deep joy in a daily walk in the park, or amazement at the afternoon spent reminiscing with Ginger, my very first friend. The willingness to continue penning my endless questions and concerns into my journal, then either sitting still long enough to listen for answers, or getting up and participating in the world around me to find them.

The eagerness to find God everywhere, in everything. The Spirit that flows through the Universe, constantly inviting us to reach out, connect, renew and live. A song, a cry, a sunrise, a new moon, a touch, a look, a painting, a poem. A phone call, an e-mail, a circle of friends, a frisky dog. Tears and laughter, pleasures and struggles, routines and new adventures, births and deaths. Emptying and filling. Round and round. Up and down. Everything.

Building on my foundation, I'm back in the public schools again, supervising new teachers in lower socio-economic schools. It's where I began 35 years ago, but this time I have thirty years of teaching experience and a manuscript of recorded anecdotes. My doctorate from the University of Life.

And I'm working with children in after school and summer programs, exploring their creativity and helping them find their voices, based on the experiences from the last six years with my own inner child.

Who am I now? There's that question again. The one that haunted me that dark January night. I am Laura — the teacher, the writer, the lover of life, the nurturing parent who knows how to nurture herself. And the voice from my pen, sounding so many times like a loving parent, has been with me as a loyal partner through this grief journey, teaching me to trust my unfolding as I write toward the Light.

I offer a final quote from Rachel Carson. "If a child is to keep alive his inborn sense of wonder, he needs the companionship of at least one adult who can share it, rediscovering with him the joy, excitement and mystery of the world we live in."

I take this as my personal challenge. I didn't know how to help my own scared child in his darkness, but the lessons I have learned from helping myself are to be shared now with others.

Further Along

May 30, 2009

When Carlton died, I was full of shame and guilt in additon to the overwhelming sadness. Maybe that's what I was calling darkness. A separation from all I once thought I knew. How could I ever face myself or others again? I'm not for real. My sense of worth was just an illusion. It distressed me to be around children. My child was gone. How unfair is that? Was this my anger stage in grief? Was I afraid of the anger I was feeling? Strong Southern ladies aren't supposed to be angry. I was out of control.

All I could do was write. I became more intimate with myself and began to feel more honest. This intimacy was like love, the unconditional kind. I know who you are and what you think, Laura, and I love you. It was the voice of God talking to a child. How could I be scared when my God-parent was so accepting of me? This new feeling made it more difficult to judge others. The light of God-love was teaching me acceptance for those so much more like me than I realized.

This laser light of truth also began burning through my knee-jerk fears, old resentments, obsolete experiences, and outdated emotions. It was cutting away unnecessary clutter, leaving the treasure of reality clearer to see.

My brother Buddy contracted viral encephalitis last year, and I visited the ICU unit daily for the month he was there. Sitting in his room, watching his swollen, comatose body hooked up to monitors and a ventilator, I had to make peace over and over again with an uncertainty I could not control. It was not easy. I would need more help.

Returning home from Bud's second day at the hospital I had an incredible urge to go to another Natalie Goldberg workshop in Taos. I called the lodge that night and signed up for a silent retreat available only to those who have studied with Natalie before. Studied with Natalie? Did I qualify? Did I think I could sit in a meditation circle in the zendo with twenty-five experienced writers? Was I good enough? Some of these people had been together many times before. We didn't talk outside the lessons. We ate meals together in silence and quietly shared rooms with others. The focus here was on something else. We were participating in a deep connection while sitting in meditation, penning multiple timed writings, and walking slowly around the room, one behind the other. Something bigger was definitely in charge. An important reminder of where this gift of writing can take me.

I also began learning new ways to use my gift of teaching. But each new opportunity presented a challenge. As I would try to leave the house, waves of naseau and noisy doubts stood between me and the kitchen door. I pushed through them. In the car without my trusty notebook, I talked loud and long to God. *Help. I don't know what I'm doing. I'm going to mess up. I can't do this by myself.*

I must have looked pretty wild driving down the street, but by the time I got to my destination I was calmer. It's the way I feel after writing. Somewhere along the way I received the courage I was asking for.

This year I taught creative play and monitored homework at a low income after-school program, facilitated a seminar for students seeking alternative certification in education at a local college, and taught creative writing to fifth graders in seven public schools. I did not actively apply for these positions. I was asked by people who knew my work. It was gratifying to find find new settings to use my gifts.

But now at the end of the day, I'm full of new experiences, images, thoughts and conversations, and sometimes this fullness can make me nervous. What's that grinding sound in my 12-year-old car? Why did that phone call irritate me? What was the uncertainty before I went to class last night?

I begin to spin. I don't have enough information; I don't know what to do. These are old reactions. Soon, however, I remember to tell myself that everything will be all right. I just need to give it time. In the morning everything will make more sense.

I knew I had to believe in something greater than myself – that what I was experiencing were not random events, and were not even that much about me. I am not in charge.

I can't spend much time now trying to second-guess what will happen, as if I could prevent all unforeseen challenges. I can't micro-analyze every conversation and event looking for answers. Surely awareness doesn't need such intense mental gymnastics. My fears made me pay close attention to everything I said and did, and I learned a lot. But now the authority of such fears has faded as they are replaced with new experiences, ideas and a sense of playful creativity. The "light" I was writing toward.

When I first wake up I still write three morning pages as described in *The Artist's Way* by Julia Cameron. It's a spiritual exercise of looking at my thoughts, dreams, and intentions. I am not alone as I work through these ideas. I am talking to God, asking for strength for my day. Asking for the next step. If I feel at loose ends during the day (my illusion of being separated), I return to my notebook.

Twice a week at Barnes and Noble's cafe, I meet friends with notebooks, pens and a timer. I value this time of shared, intimate energy. We are not alone.

Would I not know this dimension of connection if I hadn't been plunged into such darkness? Is that what this is about? Did I have to have such a traumatic wake up call? I certainly can't answer that. I've learned to call my experiences lessons. It is something my teacher-self can identify with, so I won't dwell on impossible questions like "Why me?" Instead I spend my energy as the conscientious student, wanting to please the teacher, looking for new ways to assimilate what it means and finding my place in the world.

In honor and memory of Carlton

Printed in the United States
220609BV00001B/2/P